Ethics and Values in Business Management

Ethics and Values
in
Business Management

Dr. Rinku Sanjeev

Asst. Prof (HR)
MBA dept.
Manav Rachna College of Engineering
Faridabad, (HR)

Dr. Parul Khanna

Sr. Lecturer (HR)
BBA dept.,
Faridabad Institute of Technology
Faridabad, (HR)

Ane Books Pvt. Ltd.

New Delhi ♦ Chennai

Ethics and Values in Business Management

Rinku Sanjeev and Parul Khanna

First Edition : 2014
Reprint : 2015, 2018, 2019, 2020

Published by

Ane Books Pvt. Ltd.

4821, Parwana Bhawan, 1st Floor, 24 Ansari Road, Darya Ganj,
New Delhi - 110 002, Tel.: +91(011) 23276843-44, Fax: +91(011) 23276863
e-mail: kapoor@anebooks.com, Website: www.anebooks.com

Branch Office:

- Avantika Niwas, 1st Floor, 19 Doraiswamy Road, T. Nagar,
  Chennai - 600 017, Tel.: +91(044) 28141554, 28141209
  e-mail: anebookschennai@gmail.com, rathinam@anebooks.com

ISBN : 978-81-8052-214-7

Printed at : Repro Knowledgecast Limited, Thane

Dedicated to my love ***Sanjeev*** *and kids* ***Divyansh and Manasvi***

Dr. Rinku Sanjeev

Dedicated to my love ***Manish*** *and daughter* ***Dyuti***

Dr. Parual Khanna

Foreword

The field of business ethics has traditionally been the domain of philosophers, academicians and social critics. Consequently, much of today's literature about business ethics is not geared towards the practical needs of managers-the people, primarily responsible for managing ethics in the workplace. Most of the literature on business ethics available today is a) philosophical, that requires extensive orientation and analysis; b) anthological, that requires time, review and integration; c) case studies oriented and requires time and analysis to synthesize; and d) with focus on social responsibility, that includes many examples actions taken by companies that may be right or wrong.

Ethics and values mean differently to different people. The understanding of business ethics is critical specially during times of change, faced by organizations both non-profit and profit making. During such times, values that were previously taken for granted to be correct are now strongly questioned. Many of these values are no longer followed. Consequently, there is no clear moral compass to guide managers through complex dilemmas about what is right and what is not. Awareness & importance of ethics in the workplace sensitizes both the management and the staff towards their actions. Most importantly, ethics in workplace help managers retain strong moral values specially when they are struggling in times of competition, crises and confusion. A strong ethical culture provides numerous other benefits as well, to organizations.

Information or literature on ethics and values is either not available or the one available is not well structured comprehensively in one place and thus does not create awareness amongst the concerned people to understand and realize the importance of such a critical subject.

This book addresses academician, professionals and students about the conceptual framework and several aspects of value and ethics that have not been much in discussion off late.

I welcome the authors' initiative and hope that this book will fill the much needed gap in literature in this area and help the entire professional fraternity in their working as well as personal life.

Dr. B. B. Bansal
Director- Principal
Manav Rachna College of Engineering,
Faridabad

Preface

Ethics is related to every aspect of our life. It is the set of the guiding principle for doing the right things. 'Ethics in Business' has been a hot topic and growing discipline in India. In today's corporate world, Ethics & Values in Business Management has grown to a great extent.

Ethics is a set of moral principle, which guides the code of conduct and behaviour of individual as well groups in personal and professional life and in society. Business ethics is centrally concerned with the business conduct. They are the rules of business conduct. Ethics have proved to be a controlling measure for systematic conduct of enterprises.

Ethics in business matters because there is much evidence to prove that unethical behaviour can cost a company, its reputation, affect it share price and lower its profits.

Value denotes the motive and / or basis for choosing between alternative courses of action, when an important decision needs to be taken. An organization or business has its own values, which are reflected, in the form of collective values of individuals who join it.

This book tries to bring out the relationship between ethics and values with business as well as social life. The book also gives an insight to concepts as whistle blowing, Employee Discrimination, workplace spirituality and total ethical Management. Precise and relevant discussion in simple and lucid language is the distinctive feature of the book.

The two ethical theories i.e. the virtue Theory and the utilitarian theory have also been described.

To err is human and we do not claim to be an error free. We have tried our best to put in the book. Any error or omission brought to knowledge shall be gratefully acknowledged. Besides, any suggestion made for improvement will be gratefully acknowledged.

We gratefully thank Dr. B. B. Bansal, Director- Principle- Manav Rachna College of Engineering, Faridabad for his valuable suggestion and kind cooperation.

We express our special thanks to Dr. Ravinder Vinayek, Dr. S.K.Bedi of Maharshi Dayanand University, Rohtak, Prof. A.N.Tripathi of Banaras Hindu University, Mr. P.P.Nanda and Dr. V.K.Bhatia of M.M.H.College, Ghaziabad for boosting our morale.

We heartly thank and acknowledge Dr. Kameshwar Mishra, Additional Director - L. N. Mishra College of Business Management, Muzaffarpur and Dr. Rajendra Mishra, HOD - Psychology Dept, University of Bihar, Muzaffarpur for induction of conceptual thoughts and vision which developed at this scale.

We express our deep gratitude to Mr. Sanjeev Kumar Singh, Asst. professor- Dept of Business Administration, CITM, Faridabad for his able contribution, advice and help in completing this book. We also acknowledging contribution of our parents and family members.

Last but not least we gratefully thank Mr. Sunil Saxena, Mr. Jai Raj Kapoor, Mr. Suresh and their team of **Ane Book India** in making our effort a reality.

Dr. Rinku Sanjeev
Dr. Parul Khanna

Contents

Part - I

Value: An Introduction

- Value Meaning & Nature, its Formation and Types of Value
- Value in Context of Business
- Mission Statement and Role of Corporate Values
- Relevance of Values in Management

1

Value Meaning & Nature, its Formation and Types of Values

Meaning & Nature

A value is something that has worth or importance to an individual. It contain a judgmental elemental, in that it carries an individual's ideas as to what is right, good or desirable.

Dictionary Meaning of Value is–'**Worth**', '**Merit**', '**Usefulness**', '**Importance of thing**'.

General Concept

Value denotes the motive and/or basis for choosing between alternative courses of action, when an important decision needs to be taken. Thus, values influence the process of decision-making.

According to Sociologists

'Value' has been defined as a conception of standard, cultural or merely personal, by which two or more options are compared and considered-desirable or undesirable. Our values and benefits influence to great extent, our attitudes and behaviour. High moral and ethical values lead to fair objective and decision for common good and actions that ensure the welfare of one and all.

According to Psychologists

In the words of **Milton Rokeach** – Values are global beliefs that guide actions and judgments across a variety of situations. Values represent basic convictions that a specific mode of conduct (or end-state of existence) is personally or socially preferable to an opposite mode of conduct (or end-state of existence)".

James Stoner & Freeman said, "Values are relatively permanent desires that seem to be good in them."

Values have both **Content** and **Intensity** attributes. The content attribute specifies that a mode of conduct or end-state of existence is important while the intensity attribute specifics how important it is.

Values also influence an individual's motivation and perception. That is why values are important to understand why people behave the way they do in organizational and management context.

On the basis of above definition, the following are its characteristics/ nature:

1. **Part of Culture**:– Values are elements of culture, and culture is the complex of values, ideas, attitudes and other meaningful symbols to shape human behaviour in the society. Every society has its own culture and people in that society adhere to cultural requirements.
2. **Learned Responses:**– The human beings live in a society having certain cultural characteristics, which prescribes them to behave in a particular way. Their behaviour is represented through learned experiences. The cultural field represents a set of stimuli to an individual and also a set of responses appropriate to those stimuli. The individual is either directly rewarded for adopting those responses or alternatively punished for not adopting or indirectly associated with other stimulus situations that are rewarding. Thus, through the learned experiences the individuals are uncultured or socialized. Cultural items learned early in life tend to resist change more strongly than learned late in life.
3. **Inculcated:**– Values inculcated and are passed through generation to generation by specific groups and institutions. Such transmission starts from the family from where the socialization process starts. Apart from family, educational, religious and ethnic institutions also transmit cultural values from one generation to another.

4. **Social Phenomenon:–** Values of social phenomenon, i.e. cultural habits are shared by aggregates of people living in organized society. An individual's way of thinking and behaviour constitutes culture. Group is developed and reinforced through social pressure upon those who are interacting with one another.

5. **Gratifying Responses:–** Values exist to meet the biological and other needs of the individuals in the society. Thus, elements in the culture become extinguished when they no longer are grafting to members of the society. The society rewards behaviours, which are grafting for its members.

6. **Adaptive Process:–** Culture is adaptive, either through a dialectical process or evolutionary process. Dialectical or sharply discontinuous change occurs when the value system of a culture becomes associated with gratification of only one group or class in the environment. In such case other classes of the society reject the logic of the value system and replace it with a new value system, such as through revolution or other methods.

VALUE FORMATION

Values form through different roots and sources in contemporary society. Mainly, there are five sources of value formation.

1. **Value Forming Institutions:–** The development of a human life and society is based on values. There are various institutions in the society, which inculcates values. There are four major institutions which provide the basic sources of values: - Family, School, State and Religion. These institutions teach the individuals what is good or bad for them. Good behaviour is rewarded and bad behaviour is punished. It develops and inculcates a particular behaviour.

2. **Organizational Values:–** The organization, where an individual works, affects the behaviour and shape value in working life. The different organizations have their own value system and behavioural pattern, which shapes human life.

3. **Peers and Colleagues:–** An individual learns different behaviour from his peers and colleague. In a work group an individual learn the group's norms and values. Organization or group value strengthen and protect the membership status in that group.

4. **Work and Career:-** The mode of work in an individual's career includes the task or responsibilities associated with a particular job in an organization. An individuals experience constitutes his career over a period of time. It follows a related progressive of job and stages of developments. It creates special values and norms which reflects in ideas and behaviour. Every profession has some codes of conduct, which frame professional value system.

VALUES & ATTITUDES

Some researchers see values as consisting of large sets of related attitudes. For e.g. **Fishbem and Ajzen** included three components in attitudes-informational (Ideas, beliefs and values and information), emotional (feelings of likes and dislikes or positive and negative) and behavioural (tendency to behave). Thus values are a part of attitudes.

Attitudes are specific and related to distinct objects, people or ideas: values are more general and are not related to any object or situation. They consist of statements of goodness or badness associated to the attitudes people hold. So the values are beliefs about which attitudes we should have or how we should behave.

Similarities

- Both influence behaviour of people in powerful way.
- Both are learned and acquired from the same source-experience with people and objects.
- They are relatively permanent and resistant to change.
- They have reciprocal influence and are used interchangeably.

Differences

- Attitudes reflect how one feels about something. They are learned predispositions towards aspects of our environment. Values focus on the judgment of what ought to be.
- Attitudes represent several beliefs and feelings focused on a specific object, idea, people or situations. Values, on the other hand, represent a single belief that guides actions and judgment across objects and situations.
- Attitudes and beliefs are mostly personal experiences. Values though learned from people and institutions, contain a moral flavour. Social

and cultural morals have influence on the formation of values. Values, therefore, are yardsticks to guide actions, attitudes, evaluations and justifications of the self and others'.

Types of Values

G.W. Allport, P.E.Vermon and G.Lindzey has categorized values into six major types:-

1. **Theoretical:-** Interest in the discovery of truth through reasoning and systematic thinking.
2. **Economic:-** Interest is usefulness and partiality including the accumulation of wealth.
3. **Aesthetic:-** Interest in beauty, form an artistic harmony.
4. **Social:-** Interest in people and human relationships.
5. **Political:-** Interest in gaining power and influencing other people.
6. **Religious:-** Interest in unity and understanding the cosmos as a whole.

Different people place different importance to the above six values types. In other words, every individual has a system of values ranking from first to sixth. This is important from the viewpoint of understanding the behaviour of people.

The fact that people in different occupation have different value system has led the progressive organization to improve the values-job fit in order to increase employee performance and satisfaction.

Allport suggests that a person may have different values in different degrees but he is affected more by the most important values held by him.

Graves's Classification:-

Graves has classified various personal values into 5 categories:-

1. **Existentialism:-** Orientation of behaviour congruent with existing realities.
2. **Conformistic:-** Orientation towards achievement of material beliefs through control over physical resources.
3. **Sociocentric:-** Orientation with getting along with people.
4. **Tribalistic:-** Orientation towards safety by submitting to power.
5. **Egocentric:-** Orientation to survival and power.

England's Classification:

England has classified personal values into 2 categories:-

1. **Pragmatic:** is one who takes a pragmatic view of the situation, which is stereotyped, opts for concepts and actions, which appear to him as important and successful irrespective of good or bad.
2. **Moralist:** is one who is guided by the ethical considerations of right or wrong, just or unjust, honest or dishonest.

Rokeach's Classification:

Rokeach has classified various personal values into 2 main categories:-

1. **Terminal values:** reflects what a person is ultimately striving to achieve e.g. comfortable life, family security, self-respect, achievement etc.
2. **Instrumental values:** relate to means for achieving desired ends e.g. ambition, courage, honesty, imagination etc.

Individuals differ in holding terminal values, in context to degrees. Similarly individuals may differ for achieving a particular terminal value.

2

Value in Context of Business

An organization or business has its own values which are reflected in the form of collective values of individuals who join it. The organizational values are more in the tune with the values of the managers, who frame the organizational values.

The business organizations are a part of the society. They are creatures of society and must respond to social demands. A business operates within a set of cultural norms and restraints. These restraints are not only economic but also legal, political, social and technical. As a business is a subsystem of the society, its functioning should contribute to the welfare of the system as a whole but not only to the subsystem alone. So, the organizational decisions should pertain to the total welfare of the system.

Each organization and management is considered by Indian Ethos as a living entity, having heart and soul and dharma. The traits of dharma or integrity i.e. courage, self discipline, goodness, righteousness and all other essential human and ethical values constitute the character (collective character) of management or organization. The business must follow their own dharma, (collective heart/ soul) or pay the price. A soul less company has no life.

The present role of an individual affects one's dharma. So, in the same way the dharma of the chairman and president of a business organization is different from the dharma of a clerk in the same company. Thus, each role played by one in life is different and specific. Every individual in a business firm has different roles, duties and responsibilities.

The mental contents of a good person are called moral and ethical values or we also call divine qualities. These qualities are prevalent in the employees i.e. workers, supervisors or managers of a company. However, their degree may vary. These qualities can be listed as under:-

(a) Fearlessness

(b) Courage: in the world of business, courage points out acts of bravery, e.g. deciding not to conceal something one knows and needs to be expressed openly. Guts to go ahead to take risks etc.

(c) Purity of mind and heart

(d) Integration of thoughts, action and behaviour

(e) Straight forwardness

(f) Generosity

(g) Spirit of sacrifice for the sake of common goal

(h) Inspired ideals and vision

(i) Creativity

(j) Empathy, love and affection

(k) Patience

(l) Faith

(m) Friendship with all

(n) Calmness

(o) Control of mind and restraint on senses and passions

(p) Non-violence (in ways of adopting collective largaining)

(q) Non-greediness (in terms of wages/perks etc.)

(r) Firm but fair

(s) Charity (free health care centers, adult-education etc.)

(t) Harmlessness

(u) Modesty

(v) Gentleness, truthfulness, loyalty etc.

So, a manager/worker with these values have a state of mind i.e. equanimity and he is capable to mobilize and utilize his and others energy and help accomplish all the desired aims or goals. Values are also called gunas.

Thus, the business values all these above values and tries to function and develop on the basis of these values.

In the business world, the organizations have to keep themselves away from the various unethical aspects as of:- kickbacks, double-dealings, rude behaviour and various forms of corruption and fraudulent dealings. The corruption is a world wide disease which needs to be removed.

The effectiveness at work is tried to exercising intrinsic human values i.e. moral and ethical values. These human values support established business values i.e. service, communication, excellence, credibility, innovation, creativity and coordination.

We can explore them as:

Service:-

Service can be understood as, providing the consumers or people with best product and the after sales service. The values of providing consumers with best quality product at a reasonable price are quoted. The business firm must ensure that the product sold to the masses/consumers are safe and do not include any harmful or bad ingredient, that the product is best and is being sold at a fair price tag and that the business does not create scarcity of the product i.e. the circulation of the product is appropriate to its demand etc.

Communication:-

Communication is a broader aspect and includes two parts. The first is related to the internal communication i.e. the communication with in an organization between one employee and the other. In broad meaning, it is transmission of meaning to others, it means transfer of information and understanding from person to person–a flow of information from top to the bottom and from bottom to top as well as horizontal or sideways on the same level of organization. Proper communication process helps to integrate and coordinate all managerial functions and it also links the organization with its environment and enables the enterprise to adapt to all variable force of the environment. The organization is aware of customer needs, competition, marketing opportunities, threats and risks only through effective system of communication or information. The communication process should have a Union of values and skills, which would help to eliminate any tendency to manipulate the devices of communication. Managerial leadership depends upon upward communication to the leader in the form of feedback, so as to understand emotions, feelings, motives and problem of subordinates.

William Guth and Renato Tagiuri Said, through the information gathered is filtered through manager's values and backgrounds, their values and backgrounds also inform the types of problems and opportunities they choose to work on.

The business firm should also provide right information relating to its products/services to its customers. There should not be any misleading or inadequate information relating to the products.

Excellence also relates to:-

The managers using a dynamic engagement approach pay close attention to the values that guide people in their organizations, the corporate culture that embodies those values, and the values held by the people outside the organization. Peters and Waterman from their study of "excellent" companies, found that the top performers create a broad, uplifting, shared culture, a coherent framework within which charged - up people search for appropriate adaptations. Robert Solomon argue that managers must exercise moral courage by placing value of excellence at the top of their agendas. Continually Striving towards excellence has become an organizational theme of today, as values including excellence are ethical concepts and the dynamic (changing) environment demands for it.

Innovation:-

The versatility is clearly an asset in the business. When both managers and employees can expand their roles, companies benefit and unique management practices which the other business firms may later on adopt. Creativity is the translation of a new idea into a new company. For example, Apple Computer, a new product (Sony Walkman) a new service (Federal Express's overnight delivery) a new process (one waiting line for multiple services at a bank or amusement park) a new method of production (computer-aid design and manufacturing).

Japanese are more consistent across the board in their innovative practices. They plan like demons, execute brilliantly and yet are asking how they can do better.

Credibility:-

A receiver's trust or distrust of a message is, to a large extent, a function of the credibility of the sender in the mind of the receiver. The history of work relationship is measured in terms of a manager's credibility to the message/ information. A manager's or an organization's credibility will be high if he or she is perceived by others as knowledgeable, trustworthy and sincerely concerned with the welfare of others. Credibility is the result of a long-term process in which a people/business's honesty, fair mindedness and good intentions are recognized by others. These are few shortcuts to creating a trusting atmosphere. A good rapport with the people one communicates with can only be developed through these consistent performances. So, these values are also included in the business firms.

Co-ordination:-

Co-ordination is the process of integrating activities of separate business departments in order to pursue the organizational goals effectively. The business value i.e. the co-ordination helps the employees to work effectively and efficiently so as to achieve the targets or the goals of the business. Through this value the managers are able to develop such other values as co-operation and teamwork spirit in other employees, which are also essential values of any business firm to get maximum profit.

Thus, the above of the business values are essential to achieve set goals or targets.

The human values help self-development.Various managerial functions as direction, control, supervision and communication integration and co-ordination are much easier. These values help interpersonal interactions and reduce conflicts and disputes. The business and human values are part and parcel of achieving accelerated process improvement, customer-workers and citizens satisfaction. These values enhance reputation and goodwill of the business/ organization. Through these values only the firm seeks fulfillment, happiness and success. It is a combination of inner achievement fulfillment is related to an individuals spiritual, mental, emotional and physical enrichment, whereas, the outer success fulfils the social responsibility and ecological balance and the outer success is also related to all parts of a firm's personality/image.

Due to the changing times, the enterprises in any branch of human life in India and abroad tend to disregard the importance of values. Cheating and corruption are considered essential conditions for winning.

Human, Harmony and Happiness are the main objective of any enterprise to justify its survival and progress. Ethics and Values must be an integral part of the management and work culture. But due to lack of adjustments with fast changing life and environment there is an unavoidable crisis of values – moral, ethical and spiritual degeneration. This has threatened both the physical environment and moral-ethical fabric of our society. All this has created unwanted stress ness and strains, unrest and loneliness in the human mind and adverse organizational work life. The business values should correlate with the present environmental factors. These values also plan an important role in protection of the nature. The business organization should take control over the pollution and other various environmental degradation factors. The people constitute the greatest dynamic inputs and are, the centre or pivot point and must be regarded as vital and integral part of any business organization. Every individual (employee) serves to be the representative of business values. So, the development of people or individual or employee not in skills but also in moral, ethical and spiritual values is necessary.

An employee with moral or ethical values will have poise, wisdom, harmony and peace to manage effectively others and to assure enriched quality of mind as well as enriched quality of work.

Effectiveness in performance of managers and workers is a function of business values. Every effort must be made by the top management in the business to inculcate values. The values relate to the internal domain of business that is interaction with employees, customers, suppliers, creditors, public etc.

The business values are framed and developed and are visible in the business vision, goals, objectives or in a broad way in the CORPORATE MISSION or CREED.

The business values should be followed by both the management team as well as union leaders of workers. The business should inculcate the value of giving rather than taking in work life. The business internal environment should be such that it helps to overcome the ego, to some extent selfishness, anger, jealousy, greediness, hart eyed, partiality and other such in divine elements. And the business should harness/develop all the divine elements i.e. co-operation, team spirit, trust, honesty, self-discipline, punctuality, truth and sincerity etc.

Such a kind of value driven management or business combines the requisite skills to improve the quality of work life and reputation of a corporation.

The business organizations of various countries are moving to the Indian values to neutralize the evil affects of industrialization and to synthesis human values into management and organization.

Thus, the values of the business correlates tc the following:-

Customers:-

The organization's values with reference to customer relates to the best quality of the product at fair and reasonable prices. This gives the customers fair amount of confidence in dealing with the organization concerned.

Employees:-

The employees are an integral and vital part of any business firm, so the values of business with reference to them relates to fair and reasonable wages, proper working conditions, benefits, training, health-aid etc. If these become values of any firms, then these values become guidelines for their behaviour.

Society:-

The social environment/society too demands that firm follows or adopts certain values towards the society. These relate to provision of medical hospitals, charity schools, parks, wildlife protection etc.

Industry:-

There are certain values pertaining to the industry which helps the firm to adopt and follow fair trade practices and result to healthy competition among various constituents.

3

Mission Statement and Role of the Corporate Values

Purpose or mission is a standing plan in the sense that it defines the basic intention of an organization in the light of which other actions are designed. An organization's mission consists of a long-term vision of what it seeks to do and the reasons why it exists. Its focus is on the management's concept of the organization and its contribution to the society.

The mission of an organization, when expressed in managerial meaningful terms, indicates exactly what activities the organization intends to engage in now and in future. It suggests something specific about what kind of organization it is or is to become. It depicts the organization's business character and does so in ways that tend to distinguish it from other organization.

Definition of Mission:

Mission has been defined as: - "The purpose or mission of an organization is a general enduring statement of the organization, the intent of which embodies the decision-makers philosophy. It implies the image which the organization seeks to project."

Thus, a mission statement sets basic principles and conceptual foundation upon which the corporate rests the nature of business in which it wants to participate.

Corporate mission offers guidance to the managers in developing sharply-focused, result-oriented objectives, strategies and policies. A detailed understanding of organizational mission is the starting point for rational managerial action for designing various programmes or projects, organizational process, procedure etc.

A key feature of organization's mission is that its focus is external rather than internal. **Drucker** has suggested that:-

"To know what a business we have to start with is the purpose. Its purpose must lie outside the business itself. In fact, it must lie in society since business enterprise is an organ of the society. There is only one valid definition of business purpose." To create a Customer.

Each organization has its own mission statement, which tries to reflect the value of any business/corporate sector. To achieve the mission or to maintain the values of an organization the top management determines the goals of the organizations for those who utilized the organizational resources.

Not only does the company mission embody the strategic decision-makers business philosophy or the business values, but it also reveals the image the company seeks to project. It reflects the firm's self-concept and indicates the principle, product or service areas and the primary customer needs, which the company will attempt to satisfy.

Mission of HLL

Hindustan Lever Ltd. (HLL), the company mission states that -

Hindustan Lever's commitment to national priorities has ensured that the company is a part of people's lives at the grass root level making a difference to India and to Indians - in depth, in width and in size. Hindustan Lever has always identified itself with the nation's priorities: employment generation, development of backward area, agricultural linkages, exports, contribution to exchequer etc.

Thus, every effort must be made by the top-management in the organization to inculcate values. Values relate to the internal domain of business, i.e. interaction with employees, customers, suppliers, creditors, public etc. In the corporate mission or creed we describe values, vision goals and objectives cherished by the organization.

Values should be an integral part of the corporate mission and objectives. They should be expressly mentioned in the mission document. The value orientation must be a programme-based activity. It is a long-term activity with the constant follow-up and motivation through the management support.

The corporate values of teamwork, teamspirit, unity of all efforts, mutual trust, mutual respect, personal pride, commitment, support and encouragement etc. reflect the mission statement of a corporate.

Teamwork and teamspirit, play a very important role in establishing quality management and quality environment. The Total Quality (TQ) mission will fulfill the needs and desires of the customers, both internal/ external. The mission can be achieved only through teamwork i.e. doing together. Only togetherness or unity of efforts will create and sustain an environment, where all members are self-activated toward the total satisfaction of customer needs and expectations. Each one is contributing his or her special talents and abilities to the process.

Through mutual trust, mutual respect, and personal pride and above all through genuine teamwork, the company can try utmost for the excellence or perfection. This involves constant improvements in offering our services, products and processes. The corporate employees work with dedication and devotion in every phase of the business.

The teamwork does not happen by command at a moment notice. It requires collaboration and spirit of co-operation. It needs action plan directed towards its accomplishments. The management's commitment, support and encouragement is absolutely necessary.

Teamwork represents joint action by a small team in which self-interest is subdued and unity, interest and efficiency of a team is emphasized. In essence working together, really works and firm has synergy. Teamwork can only be achieved when the management holds it gently in its hands and nurtures it in its healthy growth.

One of the latest management terms is Total Quality Management and the most important aspect of TQM is to create and maintain favourable quality environment. Mission, vision and quality - focus provides the purpose, direction, guidance, principles and charity to all employees and indicates what the firm is and what it does. The values cover the entire system and all its functions and activities.

The words in the mission statements must come to life. All the values help the corporate mission to develop the firm's profit and image as well as the esteems of a corporate sector/firms.

A mission statement is a relatively permanent part of an organization identity and can do much to unify and motivate the members of the organization and all these are the values, which enables the mission to be successful and practical.

Mission of TISCO

The fundamental mission of TISCO (Tata Iron and Steel Company Ltd.) is to strengthen India's industrial base, its increased productivity, effective utilization of manpower and material resources and continued application of modern scientific managerial methods as well as through systematic growth in keeping with national aspiration. The company recognizes that while honesty and integrity are the essential ingredients of a strong and stable enterprise, profitability provides the main spark for economic activity. It affirms its faith in democratic values and in the importance of success of individuals, collectives and corporate enterprise for the economic emancipation and prosperity of the country.

These missions of the company are directed towards making the company:-

- The best company to buy from.
- The sound company to invest in.
- A good company to work for.
- A reliable company to sell to.
- A leading company in the corporate field of the country.

Mission of ITC Ltd.

ITC Ltd., is characterized by the following concerns:-

1. Concern for their ultimate customers – millions of customers.
2. Concern for their intermediate customers – the trade
3. Concern for their suppliers – their sources of raw materials and ancillaries.
4. Concern for their employees – their most valued assets.
5. Concern for their competitors whom they wish well, for healthy competition ultimately benefit the customer.
6. Concern for their shareholders – the investing public.
7. Concern for the national aspiration – India's future.

4

Relevance of Values in Management

The human values make a man perfect and his effectiveness is reflected in his work. These human values support established business values such as service, communication in a business, school or anywhere else in the work life. Right attitude to work, principled conduct in work related activities and pursuit of value by the individual persons forming a work group are essential for uplifting the quality of work life. Manager's personal value help shaping their perception of a situation influence their analysis of alternative solution to a problem and have an effect on the ultimate decision. The followers' personal value also influences their managers.

The exploration of organizational values must be in two areas. On one side- Organization as a unit, interrelates and interacts with the external society and second side- Organization operates different functions in its internal structure.

In its relationship with the external world a good organization looks itself as an agent in the service of society. This service is performed through fulfillment of social need and realization of some values that the society considers important for its smooth functioning and growth.

Significance of Values in Management

Our effectiveness at work is tied to exercising intrinsic human values i.e. moral or ethical values. These human values support established business values such as service, communication, excellence, credibility, innovation, creativity and co-ordination.

The human values help in self-development. Managerial function such as direction, control, supervision and communication, integration and co-ordination are much easier. The human values help good interpersonal interactions. They reduce conflicts and disputes. They are part and parcel of achieving accelerated process of improvement and customer's, worker's and citizen's satisfaction. They enhance reputation and goodwill of the organization.

In the view of management and organizational work, we can say that:

- Value system influences choice of organizational goals and strategies adopted to achieve those goals.
- Value influences the way, in which an individual looks at other individual and its group of individuals that is interpersonal relationship. Value becomes basis of such interpersonal interactions.
- Individuals judge organizational success as well as its achievement on the basis of their value system.
- Individuals set limit for the determination of ethical behaviour for themselves as well as for others.
- Values determine the extent to which individuals accept organizational pressure and goals. If these do not match with their value, they throw the organizational pressure and goals and even leave the organizations.

Except this, some more points can be derived:

Value helps in Decision-making:

It helps in better decision-making because respect for ethics will from a management eye view to take all aspects into consideration, both the economical aspects and social and ethical aspects.

Essential for long-term success of Organization

An organization not responding the values and ethics can survive only for a short-period but not for long-period. An organization is required to build up a strong image for long-term survival.

Value creates credibility among Shareholders:

If values are properly followed, it would create a good image of company and it would help in attracting an immediate response of shareholders.

Value creates management credibility among Employees:

The credibility gained by top management of an ethical company and the trust generated among the employees, finally produce feeling that company does not belong exclusively to the shareholders, but rather to all the employees.

Values create credibility with the Public:

A company having the ethical and social value will be honoured and respected by even those who have no knowledge of its actual working. There will be an intuitive prejudice in favour of its product, since people believe the company gives for money.

Values are essential for long-term stability and success of business.

At last, we can say that personal and professional ethical and moral value and character alone cannot accelerate the unfolding of person's divinity. Then the psychic being, the 'Antraatma' comes forward and leads one's mental, vital and physical entities. Such a person will have poise, wisdom, harmony and peace to manage effectively to others and to assure enriched quality of mind as well as enriched quality of work.

Effectiveness in performance of managers and workers is a function of values and skills together. A good manager has strength in both values and skills. We have management by consciousness. The purity of mind and heart guides the reasoning and intellect in all managerial functions particularly in human resource management.

Every effort made by the top management in the organization, must be to inculcate values. Values relate to the internal domain of business, i.e. interaction with employees, customers, suppliers, creditors, public etc. In the corporate mission or creed, we describe values, vision, goals and objectives cherished by the organization.

An ethical management or organizational working which serve the society in realistic way has its own moral and cultural value based on social values. In modern age organizations are the driver of social ship, which floats with dignity, and sense of humour in this universe. These organizations and professionals have an urge to serve and develop the society with them and save the human as well as professionals values, which shapes humanity for the peace of mind with pleasure and this cosmic life.

Part - II

Value: An Indian Perspective

- Value System in India
- Value for Indian Managers
- Value Across Culture: Need of Value in Global Change – "An Indian Perspective"
- Secular vs. Spiritual Value
- Science and Human Values

5

Value System in India

THE PRESENT SCENARIO

In the present turbulent times there is breakdown in values. It is noticeable in almost every sphere of life. It is ranging from family, religion, administration, public life and management of corporate sector. This decline is more obvious in business industries, and public institutions, government department, voluntary organizations and professional institutions. Owing to the process of privatization, liberalization and globalization, which had come into, force in early 90's a great deal of change occurred in business scenario. Intense competition has evolved as basic guidelines for their survival. Fair competition is not bad, but unhealthy competition, which is practices in illegal way definitely is. It is simply a mad race, where each person wants to win over the other, irrespective of the consequences, which leads to the erosion of value system. Today's business world is obsessed with the idea of making profit by any means so that a vast amount of wealth can be accumulated within an incredibly short time. According to S. K. Chakraborty (1998); Present day organizations suffer from innumerable melodies driven by selfishness, egotism, pride, envy, jealously, arrogance, greed, deceit, anger, crookedness and hatred. These melodies are:

- Widespread unhappiness due to comparison with colleagues.
- Disillusionment with performance appraisal system and promotion criteria.
- Division into camps and cliques hampering fruitful communication.
- Frequent fits of anger amongst top-level officials or entrepreneurs.
- Regional prejudice.
- Glorification of speed and excitement as against serenity and harmony.
- Unreasonable personal expectations, and
- Limitless addictions to lower order material needs.

Besides these, in other areas like production, marketing, finances, govt. policies, organizational structures, a lot of malpractices are observed. Management of today is passing through a dark tunnel of corruptions, with the aim to achieve the desire results somehow or the other.

In many organizations we can see that:

- The top management has myopic view of the situation and they pressure short-term objective.
- The organization structure is not appropriate and the authority is misused to assert one-up-man ship over one another.
- There are widespread discrimination against fair sexes in terms of pay and promotion. There is a tendency to cheat customer.
- The selection of supplier and contractors is not on the basis of their competences but on sexual harassment, and other considerations.
- Inter-personal relations are based on mistrust.
- Due to lack of proper disposal of pollutant the natural environment is being polluted and health havoc is creating in society.
- Investor and shareholders are not provided with legitimate return on their investment.
- The management does not deal fair practices in recruitment, retention and reward policies.

Our whole attitude has become negative, indifferent, selfish, pessimistic, arrogant, and rigid and regulative.

So, there is need of eye-view of long-term objective with ethical and moral responsibilities by management to survive intense completion. Business people should maintain a high degree of transparency in their operations. They should provide quality products at fair price and better services should be the "Manta" for gaining customer satisfaction.

Changing Value System in India

The religious literature of India, which includes the Vedas, the different sacred books, their religious practices etc. inculcated certain individual values amongst the difference sections of the society.

The previous value system prevailing in India was basically pious (sacred) having the moral principles of respect, trustworthiness etc. but with the changing times and the upsurge of modern times, we as the Indians are now more directed by the western culture. All this led to the erosion of Indian values.

Nuclear Family:- Earlier there was the system of a close Knit family which develop the values of togetherness, sharing, respect for elders love and care for the younger ones, but with the modern developments in today the value system is directed towards the nuclear family system. The previous concepts of promise are not available in the modern time.

Punctuality and hard work:- Earlier punctuality and hardworking were the core values amongst the individuals where as in the modern era these values have been eroded.

Cut Throat Competition:- Today there is the concept of throat cut competition, which earlier was related to the fair and healthy competition. Due to the cutthroat competition the employees and the individual are forced to take up illegal and unethical practices.

Self Interest:- Today many of us are unable to see beyond our own interest. We don't care of others interest and sentiments.

Respect for Others:- Earlier they used to respect each other very much. They used to treat guests as God. But now no more the people are concerned about others. They respect only those with whom they feel it would be beneficial for them in respect of money matters. They respect an individual for their profit and, in actual they hate person on his back and don't even like to talk with that person.

Sincerity towards Work:- Earlier people were sincere toward their work. But today value system has changed. Now, no longer people are sincere. They don't learn to work. They are work shinkers. There are just concerned about the salary or the wages, which they are going to earn. They want to earn without performing any task.

Simplicity:- Earlier the life style was very simple. People believed in simple living and high thinking. They used to wear cloths for covering their body, but now the mentality has totally changed. They wear cloths, which attract others. They believe in exposure.

Non-violence:- Earlier people believe in non-violence. But now there is a lack of tolerance. People have become hot-blooded. They always ready for fight at every moment.

Responsibility:- Responsibility was the core value of the traditional individuals. The success or the various of any task used to lie on the traditions man's hard work, punctuality and sincerity. However, this concept has changed wherein people take responsibility only for the success but not for failure of any work.

Sharing the credit:- The traditional value system also witnessed the value of 'share the credit' which means that when a group of people work together and achieves some success then they used to share the success with each other. But in the modern scenario, this value has changed i.e. group leader, team leader wishes to have the full credit of the success so as to gain maximum benefits of promotion, appreciation, awards, monetary rewards etc.

Differentiation between girls and boys:- In the past there was a system of differentiation between boy and girl. But it now no longer exists except in least developed area like villages. Earlier girls were not allowed to go out for studies but now the total scenario has changed. Now girls are treated equal to boys. They go for study. They have the same status in society as that of boy.

Labour Intensive Approach:- Earlier most of work was done by hand. It was an age of labour intensive approach but now with commencement of new technology this system has totally changed. With the advancement in techniques and computerized technology it has been made capital intensive.

Education System:- Earlier the method of study was knowledge oriented. The people study to take care for the social welfare of society. Now it has been career oriented. New courses and methodology have been evolved, which provides new areas of career.

Family Composition:- There is also a change in family concept. Earlier in one family only one person was livelihood earner and people have so many children. But now there is a concept of DINK (double income no kids) and DIOK (double income one kid). The people have become career conscious. They don't have time for taking care of children.

Workplace Culture:- The term culture consists of such values as defined under the word 'OCTAPACE'. Wherein 'O' stands for Openness, 'C' stands for Cooperation, 'T' stands for Trust, 'A' stands for Authority, 'P' stands for Participation, 'A' stands for Autonomy, 'C' stands for Collaboration, 'E' stands for Empathy.

These values are more prevalent in the traditional workplace as compared to the modern workplace.

Consumer Awareness with regard to Product Quality:- In the traditional era, the customers were quality conscious but in modern era, the customer have a shift from Product Quality to Product Quality. People today are ready to pay more for a good Quality Product.

Humanity and Ethical Basis:- Earlier people believe in humanity. There was a sense and feeling of brotherhood. But now this mentality has been changed. There is no sense of humanity. People behave like machines they believe in professionalism.

Concluding, it can be said that changing life style and professionalism has changed the whole concept of life. In this competitive commercial age people have no time to think over the ethical and social concerned. Every body is in hurry to go ahead. An urge of fast speed has pushed every ethical concern back. People have no care of others but even sometimes not for themselves when there is target-oriented approach. This led to the change in whole value system. Our value system has been influence by western culture, the society has been moving towards that stage of development from where even the western people are looking back. It is the requirement of present time that we should look back also towards our traditional value system which has been the guide of Indian heritage as "WORLD GURU".

6

Value for Indian Managers

Value refers the in-built mechanism, which distinguishes the right from the wrong. Right or wrong can not be interpreted in absolute sense but only in context of the social environment in which an individual lives.

An organization has its own ideals of business, which are reflected in the form of collective values of the individuals, who work in that organization. Nowadays the organizations want to employ and develop only those people, who possess a special predefined set of competencies i.e. creativity, innovation, adaptability, teamwork, personal integrity etc. These competencies ensure that the organizational goals will be achieved in tune with corporate culture and values.

Managers create a special influence, as they participate in formulating business strategy and decision-making process. They are directly responsible in meeting planned organizational objective. The organizational values are more in tune with the values of the managers who frame it. Managers are a part of a society as they are also the human beings. They are creatures of the society and they must respond to the social demand, which reflects in social values.

Value held by managers provides guidelines for how employees can expect to be treated. Managerial values are the set of conscience driven factors and those qualities, which influence decisions and work commitment with organizational culture and goal.

Management was once a personal and direct actions. It has now grown into an indirect phenomenon. This changed in management system has brought in a lure for materialism and the race of production and distribution has brought for a lust for profit all round. The maximization of profit becomes the ultimate goal. There is a blind race through manipulation and control over the market.

In this context managerial value can be categories in three parts in an organizational environment.

1. Physical values
2. Organizational values
3. Psychological values

1. Physical Values

- **Accuracy:**

The precision, exactness and conforming to the fact in details of work.

- **Cleanliness:**

In offices, production and warehouse facilities, equipments, customer service areas, raw material and finished product inventory, bathrooms and so on.

- **Maximum utilization of resources:**

The desire and ability of the company to improve its performance by full utilization of its current resources. (Time, money, equipment, material, space, people etc.

- **Orderliness:**

In offices drawers file cabinets, shelves, paper work, files, phone numbers, priority of work, daily and weekly plan.

- **Punctuality and Timeliness:-**

In arriving on time to work, from breaks, from lunch, to meetings, in replying to letters and phone calls, in paying bills on time, etc. Occurring at the most suitable or opportune time.

- **Quality of Products and Services:-**

In terms of presentation, functionality, choice, value, speed, timeliness, suitability, repeatability, reliability, life span, courtesy, friendliness, etc.

- **Regularity**

Of meeting, reports, sales calls, performance reviews, and so forth

- **Reliability**
- **Responsiveness**

The way people, the organization, systems, etc. react to a need coming from within or from outside the organization.

- **Safety**

In office, warehouses, production and research facilities, vehicles, for employees, vendors, and customers.

- **Speed of operations**
- **Time**

2. Organizational Values

- **Accountability**

Of individuals, departments and division for performance, results, problems and so on.

- **Communications**

Up, down, and sideways with in the company, with customers and vendors, in terms of openness, frankness, clarity, frequency, accuracy, timeliness, and brevity.

- **Cooperation (Teamwork)**

Among individuals, departments, divisions, branches and so on

- **Coordination**

Horizontally between departments in terms of plans, activities and systems.

Discipline in adherence to company policy, rules, systems, procedures, schedules, standards, ethics, and so on.

- **Freedom for Initiative**

To make suggestions, develop plans, make decisions, carry out or modify actions, and so on.

- **Integration**

For smooth operation vertically between different levels of the organization in terms of plans, decisions, priorities.

- **Standardization**

In terms of forms, files, procedures, reports, performance evaluations, equipment, training, recruitment, orientations, communications, and so on.

- **Systemization**

In sales, marketing, customer service accounting, research, production, engineering, recruitment, training, promotions, communications, coordination, reporting, and so on.

3. Psychological Values

- **Continuous improvement**

The desire and ability of the company to develop and incorporate ways to improve itself.

- **Creativity**

In terms of new products, new ideas, new systems, new production methods, new applications of technology, new methods of financing, new marketing strategies.

- **Customer delight**

The positive emotional response and joy that the customer feels from interaction with our people and our products and services.

- **Decisiveness**

In solving problems, planning, executing plans in terms of speed and commitment to decisions once made.

- **Develop people**

The desire and ability of the company to improve the lot of the employees working for it.

- **Harmony**

The overall atmosphere and interaction between people, departments, divisions, systems, activities, rules, and policies within the company and between these elements and the external environment, customers, vendors, community laws, and so on.

- **Innovation**

The desire and ability of the company to venture into new, breakthrough areas of opportunity.

- **Integrity**

Keeping to one's word, promises, agreements, being truthful, non-deceitful etc. with employees, customers, vendors, government etc.

- **Loyalty**

To and from suppliers, customers, and employees.

- **Respect for the individual**

In establishing rules and policies, design of systems, making decisions, executing instructions and so on in terms of people's health, safety, self esteem, feelings and opinions.

- **Service to society**

Community welfare, environmental protection, development of products and services that meet real physical, social, or psychological needs are the primary activities of managers.

Value for Managers in India

Values of managers depend on socio-cultural factors obtaining in a given society.

(a) Core Values of Managers in India

There may be divergent values in tune with the nature and goals of different functional departments and also the overall organizational culture. However, there are some dominant values also known as core values that are considered as crucial by majority of managers:

- Integrity
- Trust
- Achievement Motivation
- Truthfulness
- Humility and Contentment

(b) Personal Traits of Managers in India

Personal traits are enduring characteristics of an individual by which he/she can be identified and also to a certain extent differentiated from others. Every manager has certain personal traits which make him/her successful and efficient. The respondent executives indicated that the following are the dominant traits:

- Stability
- Skill
- Creativity
- Achievement
- Flexibility

(c) Goals of a Typical Manager in India

Values of a manager will have a direct influence on the goals and objective he sets. Personal goals of a manager may vary depending on goals, culture and philosophy of the concerned organization. Nevertheless, each manager works with a certain aim and purpose in his mind. The following are the goals of a typical manager in India:

- Customer satisfaction
- Achievement of departmental and organizational goals
- Completion of tasks within scheduled time frame
- Employee motivation
- Career progress

(d) Important Personal Qualities of a Manager

Managers with limited abilities and skills, with static values and goals may not be able to achieve success in all circumstances. Certain personal qualities (height, complexion, voice, dressing habits, gregariousness, versatility, etc., should supplement and stand in good stead of an individual supplement and stand in good stead of an individual to accomplish all-round success. The respondent executives reported that the following five qualities are important for a typical manager in India today:

- Self control
- Articulation abilities
- Sociability
- Physical stature
- Dress

(e) Private Values of Managers

Private values of a manager refer to all those values which he holds while undertaking activities besides organizational responsibilities. If an individual daily goes for a walk in the morning, it is a value, and if he/she spends an hour every night helping the child doing the homework gives by the teachers at school, it is a value. Therefore, all the other roles that a manager has to play, called private life values. All those who hold important position in an organization acknowledge that their life mostly revolves around organization and organizational related activities. However, there is a small proportion of managerial workforce who ignores organizational responsibilities and work for the promotion of personal interests.

Values thus provide an individual with standards for taking action, for justifying one's own and other's actions, and for comparing the self with others. An understanding of one's own inner mechanism that impetus himself to think, speaks, and acts in a particular manner which remains otherwise unconscious and thereby inaccessible. Over a time an individual develops a set of values and also an order among them by means of socialization which becomes his/her value system. Values are important in business because they provide bases for decisions and action.

7

Value Across Culture: Need of Value in Global Change- "An Indian Perspective"

Today we have entered in 21st century; we are running in the age of globalization. We are trying to go hand with both eastern and western society. It is time to pick up the right path and right view of personal and professional life. When we talk about values, we see too much up and down in our value systems. Sometimes we see the Deepings value crisis in contemporary Indian society even after fifty years of progress in different fields like – economic, industrial and scientific platform, it is doubtful if we are moving towards creation of a happy society or a good society. At the time of independence, we gave ourselves a thoroughly enlightened, constitution for the creation of a good and modern society but have we achieved this goal? The concept of good life has been restricted to very narrow confines. Good life is one with unrestricted enjoyment of sensuous pleasures and fulfillment of unlimited desires.

In the time of dependence and pre war years India learned the technique of modern management mostly from the United Kingdom. In the past war years India turned to the United States in this and many others spheres of knowledge and techniques. Now we are leaning it from many other nations as well.

As we are entering deeper and deeper into the processes of modern industrialization, the subject of management is assuming increasing importance. We are facing the problems of tackling efficiently the organization and management of our ever-expanding development monetary investment of our material resources and workforce. There is a quick transition taking place in our expanding industry from hereditary to professional management cadres. This has called for the need for management trainee for the fulfillment of which more and more institute and schools of management are coming up in all the parts of our country.

Management should try to develop human values by setting examples so that they are perceived as role models. We can summarize the need or role of value in creating motivation development and interpersonal relationship with different groups.

1. Value Creation for Work Force:

An organization culture should create a sense of commitment in the workforce. They must love their job and should be dedicated to their work. For this dedication a personal should feel as a member of family where there is no bounding but freedom and opportunity to develop him as well as the organization. In consideration of this view the management should take some steps as:

- Taking the initiative to implement a meaningful that address personal basis and values that foster harassment of individuals.
- Developing and implementing programme that strive to change behaviours not just attitude.
- Securing commitment from top management at all level of efforts.
- There should be no discrimination or degradation at multiple level of the structure in terms on pay and promotion.
- Proper alertness programmes should be conducted among women employees.

2. Value Creation for customers:

Owing to globalization and liberalization, Indian economy has brought intense competition for business organization. The survival of the organization depends upon the necessary expertise and capability to satisfy global markets.

Grouping awareness of customers about their needs and rights is changing their behaviour. Customer is becoming increasingly assertive in demanding high quality products and services.

These customers should be treated as reigning deity-company should maintain high degree of transparency in their operation product or services and related information to the customer.

3. Value Creation for Investors and Share holders:

Shareholders and investors are company-owners. They expect proper return on their investment. So, the company should provide detail information regarding expenditure and overall performance of the company. Fair and ethical treatment should be provided to them in the following manner:

- The money invested by them should be judiciously used.
- No personal expenditure should form part of the investor's money.
- The management should provide detailed information regarding expenditure.
- Proper return and dividends must be given.

Thus, for effective value based governance, organizations need to have a code of conduct which the company should follow, while dealing with internal and external stakeholders, to whom the company is accountable.

4. Value creation for society:

Organization exists within the society and their members are come from the society. Every society has its own value and names. Similarly the organization has its own values and norms towards society. Here, business organizations are expected to play a leading role in solving the social problems. They should not create nuisances. Proper measures should be taken for disposal of industrial pollutants. They should take care of their physical and environmental problems also. Social obligations are to be properly discharged by the business organizations. So, that the society can develop at all level human task and performance.

They long-term viability and progress and all round development of a nation depend not so much on its material, primarily it depends on its material ecological or technological resources but primarily it depends on its human resources having ample potential energy that is spiritual and psychological resources of our people. As a manager or as a worker a human being is primarily a spiritual and psychological resource. In the other words - a soul and a mind work here much. Spirituality is the essence of our national vitality. The vitality of Indian wisdom and culture lies in its creative and progressive and endeavour in spiritual, science, thought and practice. We have to maintain this creative and progressive attitude to our unique, genius and wisdom for the progress and development of India and the humanity as a whole.

8

Secular vs. Spiritual Value

Secularism

The word secular refers the worldly things that are physical not religious.

Secularism refers to rational or knowledgeable working for the livelihood of a person. You can also call it professional working which is completely apart from the difference of caste, colour, nature, sex, religion or any other such basic differences of human beings. This quality turns an individual to a professional or a secular human being.

Spirituality

Spirituality refers to the concept of soul or the feelings what we have in our inner heart. Out of the limitations of physical life there is a limitless world, where a person work from his real satisfaction or inner satisfaction and, for satisfaction of others. The things, which really affect human being, are called spiritual things. This concept of spiritualism is not understandable or acceptable for all the people, but we should say that it is a mystery for most of the people in our society. They either do not know or ignore these things because of the glorious environment of the physical life.

The values, which are followed or are in mind for both the concepts are very different in nature.

Secular Business Value

1. **Productivity:** Business value emphasis on productivity through which an organization serve the society. It doesn't make any difference on the basis of caste, religion or any other difference of customer.
2. **Profit:** Business is done for profit for the organization by which it can survive and develop. This profit should be justified in context of service and development of society.
3. **Goodwill and Reputation:** Goodwill is the most important things for the business people. All the customer of any society should be satisfy from the services of any organization. It makes an organization a real unit of service-oriented industry.
4. **Responsibility:** Business people and organization are equally responsible to the whole society for the safe development and harmony.
5. **Strategy and Achievement:** All the professionals of an organization have their strategy for achieving their goal and objective to serve the society and make profit again for the development.

Characteristics of Secular Values

1. Focus on factual realities: in secular value system approach the facts of life are the major source of inspiration and not the religious way.
2. It treats the person on the basis of actuality.
3. Secular values focuses on practical orientation and independent efforts.
4. These values focus on scientific facts.
5. These values believe in equality: it emphasis that there is no superior or inferior caste; in the same way there is no superior or inferior religion. All human beings are equal and should be treated in the same manner.

Spiritual Managerial Value

1. **Self Fulfillments:** Spiritual persons should have a feeling of self-completeness. They should have no personal desire or goal where they seek any thing any body. They should not deficit driven personality.
2. **Ego-less Ness:** Spiritual persons have a concept of unity of all life. They don't have a sense of separate or individual existence where they feel egoistic. They see themselves in all and all in themselves.

They don't have greed, anger, jealousy or any other such bad feelings, which made differences. **Ego is the cause of all the evils.**

3. **Complete freedom :** Spiritual people are free from all human limitations or personal attachments. They have over come all dualities conflicts and suffering of life. So they are living a blissful life from heart and soul.
4. **Universal or unconditional love:** Spirituality loves all the human being. It is concern for the sharing, caring and giving out their humanness to others their conduct and behaviour are guided by the ethics of love. They don't have any fear from anyone and no body has any fear from them. This is called the great spiritual value of 'Abhaya'.

Characteristics of Spiritual Values

1. Consciousness: The spiritual value for managers suggest on having a higher level of consciousness, which means that a manager must be aware of positive and negative effects of his action and decisions undertaken, which are consciously performed.
2. Wisdom and skills: Any act performed by a person must follow an approach of wisdom which has always support of spirituality and is automatically get reflected in the skills. For example, if a manager believes in the principle 'Every soul has a potential of God in it' than all the skills he practice and exhibits get reflected in his deeds. With this belief he would enjoy his life more purposefully.
3. Spiritual values in terms of divine qualities: There are number of divine qualities which are present in an individual and can be termed as spiritual values e.g. respect for self, respect for god, belief in giving than grabbing, enjoying satisfaction to its maximum level. All these factors present the divine qualities.
4. Spiritual values in terms of inspiration and purification. High level of inspiration can be achieved through any of the source of life. Purification in terms of value means purification of heart, feelings and expression. Inspiration can be achieved through God or may be form of any living or non-living objects.
5. Strong belief in religion: The way we behave is the reflection of our religion on a broader level. People being different follow different religion, respect different god that leads to a moral strength in them. As has rightly been said, 'belief in religion is a mirror of our spiritual values'.

6. Karma Yoga: To be able to perform one's responsibility and duties properly, is a major source of inspiration.
7. Control over mind: It is another important features in terms of our spiritual values. So right from the childhood one must be taught to keep a control and balance over the mind and learn to behave in the family as well as society. Control over mind also helps in proper usage of pure energy and resources. Aim is to attain a state of pure mind.
8. Balance between need, wants and demand: The most important factor in terms of spiritual value is to maintain a balance between need, wants and demand. The most satisfied person is the one who has a clear idea about his expectations from life and accordingly identifies what are his need, wants and demands are.

Spirituality makes one to

- Love and be concerned about everything in nature including all animals and plants.
- Recognize that all other beings have life, feelings, thoughts, hunger etc.
- Remain less arrogant about self.
- Become more humble.
- Be inclined to do more good than hate to others.
- Be selfless, compassionate, kind, charitable etc.
- A void exploiting or cheating others.
- Be concerned about the environment.
- Recognized that one's success is to be seen in terms other than material.
- Pay attention to the effect of processes and product with regards to their safety and harmfulness.
- Respect warranty and other promises made while doing business.

Secular vs. Spiritual Working

1. Secularism talks through word. Spiritual talks through inner feeling.
2. Secularism work as professionalism. Spiritualism work as humanism.
3. Secularism is primarily profit oriented. Spiritualism is primarily satisfaction oriented.

4. Secularism bears responsibility towards organization. Spiritualism bears responsibility towards society and world.

Although secular and spiritual values seems opposite in nature and refers to two different approaches to working life, there may be combined humanistic, cultural, religious and spiritual ideals in attitude and behaviour as well as in thought and actions. By adopting this approach a manager can develop a holistic approach. In this way he can enhance and beautify his personality. With such attitudes and attributes a manager can develop as good association and respect with his family members, bosses, colleagues, subordinates and society. It will increase his managerial performance and moral excellence.

At this stage he will not have such tension or anxiety, worry, guilt, nervousness or diffidence. His confidence and courage will be developed which improves the decision-making process. So, there is a need to get the opportunity for changing the organizational culture. Most of managers do not have this opportunity, unless one is at the top level with power for influencing the values of the organization. It can be said that the man with such power can enhance the power of authority, derived from hierarchy, money, articulation and ability in positive direction.

9

Science and Human Values

From the Vedic age our Gurus are concerned about the right utilization of resources and power we have. In the Mahabharata, it is said that Guru Dronacharya rewarded Arjuna with supreme weapon Brahmastra. But he did not give it to his son Ashwathama. He was against to give this most sophisticated weapon to his own son because he was afraid that Ashwathama might misuse it as he has high skills but low values.

Some others social thinkers have also questioned it time-to-time. Guru Tagore was worried about moral problems in the age of scientific development. He said, "Our Scientific world is our world of reasoning. We are ready to pay to the homage due to it but the reality of the world belongs to the personality of man and not to the reasoning which is useful and great though it be, is not man himself."

Sarvpalli Radhna Krishnan said, "In a technological civilization, in a mass society the individual becomes a depersonalized unit. Things control life. Statistical average replaces qualitative human beings. In his view, science and technology has undermined mankind's incentives for self mastery and aggravated his mental restlessness."

Gandhiji pointed out the ethical flaws of mechanization from the wider social perspective. He said "I refused to be dazzled by the seeming triumph of machinery. I am uncompromisingly against all destructive machinery. But simple tools and instruments and such machinery as saves individual labour and lightens the burden of million cottages, I should welcome." According to him, "High thinking is inconsistent with complicated material life based on high speed imposed on us by Mammon worship. All the graces of life are possible only when we learn the art of living nobly."

In the ancient time, these questions did not arise much, because there hardly were such consequences. In those days science had very little concern in the day-to-day life of people. There was no computer then. No internet facility was there. People used to communicate their observation to other people with similar hobbies at gathering of social function.

Gradually, in course of time science began to be taken up as full time profession. So many clubs and societies of science were established. This widened even further the detachment of scientists from society. The detachment of scientists from general human affairs led them to build an ivory tower in which they sheltered. Their works were now separated from the human welfare.

The tremendous advancement in pure science in 20th century has completely changed the relation between science and society. Science has become a dominant element in our lives. It has brought great improvements in the quality of life, but also grave perils.

It created pollution of the environment, squandering of vital resources, increase in transmittable diseases, which are threat to the existence of the human species on this planet especially through the development of nuclear weapons.

Now a day, we are in a world community with ever greater independence which has been gifted through technical advancement arising from scientific research. An interdependent community offers great benefits to its members but the same time it also imposes some responsibility on them. Every citizen has to be accountable for his or her deeds. Everybody has a responsibility to society and this includes scientists too, who are first and foremost citizens. Indeed, this responsibility goes heavily on scientists particularly because they play a dominant role in the society. They understand the technical problems better than the other citizen.

The fulfillment of the social responsibility needs to take certain measures. There is the need for action for the universities to introduce an awareness programme at science degree ceremonies. This is very important that new comers in a scientific career become aware their social responsibility. It is also important that senior people acknowledge their own awareness of such responsibilities. The committees of eminent scientist from different disciplines should be setup for the task of examining potentially harmful long-term effects of proposed research projects. Such project should be reviewed.

Two more aspects of ethics in science seem contradictory. These need to be examined. These are: - Whistle-blowing and Irresponsible publication.

The first is related directly from the social responsibility of scientists. If in the course of work in a governmental or private organization, a scientist becomes aware of an undisclosed application which is harmful for society, it must be their duty to disclose it to the concern authorities and to if possible to the general public, so that a preventive action can be taken. At present, this practice is rather dangerous. The whistle-blower is subject to reprisals, dismissal from their job or even more severe punishment. This legislation or practice should be revised and amended, to provide immunity to whistle-blowers.

The other practice where some scientist publishes results of research, that are based on insufficient data or erroneous interpretation, which may have an impact on society. Sometimes those publications are not through a scientific journal where it would have to pass peer review, but directly in a release to the media. The general public believes in sensational findings. It may lead to a great deal of suffering. The case becomes worse when the concerned scientist persists with the finding, are shown to be false.

The big negative aspect of scientific research is the extent to which it has became motivated by financial gain. The financial promoters of research projects, particularly in the pharmaceutical industry, influence the publication of findings, either prohibiting publication or considerable delay. The whole concept of patenting scientific findings goes against a basic tenet of science. It also affects the pursuit of science by earning money for the use of essential materials, or the technology covered by patent rights. To overcome these inequities, some action should be taken. It may be in form of banning the grant of patents for certain results of scientific research, especially on basic materials.

Thousands of scientists are employed in big organization, doing pure and applied research for specific purpose, purposes those seem as the negligence of scientific pursuit. The development of new, or improvement of old weapons of mass destruction is major in these research. Among these thousands of scientists, these may some, who are motivated by consideration of national security. The vast majority have no such motivation. They are working by the name of scientific advancement and development. These things must be considered for ethical and point of view for the sake and betterment of humanity.

So, the time has come for some kind of oath, to be taken scientists particularly when receiving a degree in science. Atleast it would have a sense of moral and ethical values. It might also generate awareness and stimulate the thinking pattern on this wide issue.

Part - III

Ethics : An Overview

- Meaning, Nature, Determinants & Objectives and Work Ethics
- Ethics and its Relation to— Values, Norms and Morals
- Teaching Ethics
- Holistic Approach in Decision Making
- Virtue Theory
- Utilitarian Theory
- Utilitarianism and its Application to Business

10

Meaning Nature, Determinants & Objectives and Work Ethics

Every individual of this world wants to live in an ideal world, where he seeks to determine the norms, ideals and standards of the particular society or organization. It is generally observed that there are three ideals of human life, i.e. Truth, beauty and goodness. They correspond to three aspects of our experiences—thinking, feeling and willing. The ideals of good refer to the ethics.

Ethics is the subject of philosophy. It refers to the standards on which the person decides what is right or wrong or good or bad. It prescribes what human being ought to do, usually in terms of rights, obligations, benefit to society, fairness or specific virtues. It also refers to the study and development of one's ethical standards if they are reasonable and justified enough or not. It means Ethics is the activity of examining the moral standards of an individual and a society and asking how these standards apply to our lives and whether these standards are reasonable or unreasonable i.e. whether they are supported by good reasons or poor ones.

So, it can be said that **Ethics is a set of moral principles, which guides the code of conduct and behaviour of a human being in his life and in society.** It is person's own attitude and concerning good behaviours. It resides within individuals and each individual in his own way defines these separately.

Nature of Ethics

- Ethics is a subject that deals with human being.
- Ethics is a social as well as individual phenomenon.
- Ethics is perceived as Science than Art - there was an argument whether ethics is a science or an art. But thinkers found that it is more of a science than art because it is a defined and systematic knowledge about moral behaviour and conduct of human being. It is a normative science, which implies a guide or control of action.
- Ethical standards are the ideals for conduct of life - it reflects the moral philosophy of the culture for a society. It deals with human conduct that is voluntary and forced by any person's circumstances.

Determinants of Ethics

There are several key forces and factors, which shape the code of conduct and behaviour of a society and individuals. These may be stated as:

1. **Value and morals:** The code of conduct is based on the value and morals of a person or a society, which leads to setting of goals and objectives and the effort for achieving these levels.
2. **Family, schools and religions:** The learning of behaviour starts in the beginning of one's life. In the family one learns what is good or bad, what ought to do or not to do. The parents and family members inculcate the value, morals and ethical standards among their children by rewarding good behaviour and controlling unacceptable manners. In the same way, a student learns several behaviours from school and religious society. It may be in terms of truthfulness, honesty, sincerity, tolerance etc.
3. **Peers, Colleagues and Superiors:** A person learns most of the behavior of life from his workplace. The friends, team members and superior people promote, rewards and control the different behaviour, which develops a pattern of working.
4. **Social pressure:** There is a considerer able influence of social pressure on the life style of a person. The different customs, norms, culture, beliefs of a society. Discrimination based on caste system, different boycotts (for products, person or society), prevention for the construction of any such thing like nuclear power plant, ban on adoption for social reformation (like widow marriage, sati pratha) restrict the thoughts as well as actions in one's life.
5. **Experiences from life:** One learns so many lessons from his own experiences from his own life. There may be so many bitter or sweet

experiences depending on the ability of a person or expectation. Success or failure teach how to do or act next in an individuals life.

6. **Organizational demand and ethical codes:** The organizations have their specific guidelines for the managers as well as employees. The employees as ethics of the organization follow these codes of behaviour. All the top, middle and first level management compromise their personal principles to meet the organizational demand. The corporate goals and objectives exert considerable pressure of the executive to change their ethical views.
7. **Legislation:** Govt. legislation, rules and regulations guide the code of conduct about ethical standards, social responsibilities, exploitation, corruption in public life, product safety, working condition, statutory, warning etc. these guidelines helps in determining what are acceptable standards and practices.
8. **Threatened situations:** There are several situations in a person's life where he or she faces several threats. It may be loss of job, social boycott, critical disease, loss of wealth etc. which bounds human behaviour and sets the new path of conduct for personal and professional life.

Objectives

- To set the standard of personal life and norms of behaviour.
- To define the working pattern of professional life.
- To set a standard for do's and don'ts.
- To develop a value system.
- To create strong work culture.
- To set the mission of life.
- To inculcate good behaviour in children.
- To improve the social life.
- To balance the need and wishes of human being.
- To prevent the social evils.

Work Ethics

Work Ethics is a set of moral principles or accepted norms of behaviour governing the conduct of a group of persons involved in some work situation to achieve certain desired objectives.

Why should we concern ourselves with Ethics in Work?

Most people want to live in a good society. One fundamental characteristics of good society is that justice and charity prevail there. There if we consider ourselves good persons, we must the responsibility of helping the society. So, it can be perfect and this perfection should start with our perfection. Every human being has got some negative characteristics, but some characteristics are treated as very bad such as cheating, stealing, telling lies is not exactly forgotten or forgiven in business world.

Almost everyone should have compassion for someone, no one excuse immorality. In modern business environment, when the globalization has spread all over the world, the need for commonly accepted ethical standards as taken on new dimensions of even greater importance.

Dimension of Work Ethics

1. Rightful Expectations

- Work ethics refer to ethical attitude to work alone in context of employment.
- In any organization, efficient and diligent performance of duties assigned to the employees.
- This is rightful expectations and moral demand on the employee of the employer.
- An employer gives an opportunity, career and a status to an employee.
- So, the employee should give out his or her best to the organization. This is **ethical demand of duty**.
- Shrinking work, making excuses for poor performance, finding faults with organization etc. are against the demand of work ethics.
- On the other hand, in the same way employee also has rightful expectation from the employer.
- It is regarding their service condition for career advancement and recognition and reward, for their work. So this is called ethical employee-employer relationship.

2. Sense of Loyalty towards the Organization

Loyalty means safeguarding and promoting the interest of the organization. It requires a sense of devotion and allegiance beyond the routine job requirement and duties. A loyal employee should not promote those personal interests which are competing organization at the cost of organization. He acts as a faithful agent promoting organizational goals. Loyalty also means giving organizational needs a higher priority over personal needs.

3. Discipline

Every organization and work group have written or unwritten rules, norms and ways of working. The members or employees have to follow them. There is a hierarchy of power and authority at the work. The people on lower level are expected to follow orders, directions and suggestions given by their superiors. Obeying the orders is a part of discipline.

On the other hand, there should be no harassing environment for lower level people.

There should be mutual trust, respect and friendly relations between each other. A good organization must provide appropriate channels for grievance redressal and for investigating complaints against its higher-level executives.

The higher authority should know sense of responsibility. It should be utilized humbly for promoting the goals of organization, to motivate and help subordinates in their self growth and to provide initiative and leadership for collective growth.

Work Ethics in Management

There are two aspects of management function

(i) Effectiveness

(ii) Efficiency

Effectiveness is doing the right things.

Efficiency is doing things right.

We can sum the management function as:-

1. Forming a vision and planning the strategy to realize such vision.
2. Cultivating the art of leadership.
3. Establishing the institutional excellence and building and organization.
4. Developing human resources.
5. Team building and team work.
6. Delegation, motivation and communication.
7. Reviewing performance and taking corrective steps whenever required.

So, we can say that Management is a process in search of excellence to align people and get them committed to work for a common goal to the maximum social benefit.

In business environment, the organizations try to structure the code of conduct or norms of behaviour in defined manner i.e. Do's and Don'ts. Some Do's and Don'ts in a business set up can be summarized as -

Do's: To do things that are morally good or right. For example

Punctuality

Courtesy

Efficiency

Hard work

Sincerity

Devotion to duty

Regularity

Discipline

Promptness

Initiatives etc.

Don'ts: To restrain from doing that is morally wrong or bad. For example

Insubordination

Lethargy

Corruption

Dishonesty etc.

It can be observed, **"Work Ethic embraces work responsibility, work conscience, ethical work conduct. If one has the satisfaction that he is contributing his very best to his organization and is not just earning the bread, then this would be the true feeling of work ethics. Work Ethic demands that one works for attaining organizational objectives in its fullest measure."**

4. P's of Work Ethics

Whenever an individual joins an organization he/she is under an obligation of job contract, which confers a right to be duly compensated against what he is committed to perform. To fulfill his obligation and committed he is expected to preserve certain degree of skills and attitudes such as regularity, punctuality, discipline, initiative etc. All these together combine an ethical value system which every employee must follow however sometimes organization's atmosphere may be different. Even then an individual is expected to be ethical at his own level.

Generally at workplace, people are concerned for three factors or 3 P's i.e. Pay, Prospects, Promotion but one 4th P i.e. Performance is the most important factor which determines the organizational as well as personal development.

Ethics: The Standard for Moral Judgments

The work life can't move with only a feeling or desire of wants. When a person is moving towards action, he must have the conception of the end result to be attain. The motive, which induces to a person to act, is the thought for satisfaction of desire and wants. This thought initiate a decision-making process for what, how, when to do. It is also a process of selecting the right alternative from the several options between do's and don'ts, here the ethics represents a process of moral judgments. Both personal and professional ethics act as stimulator and controller for action, attitude and behaviour of a person. Sometimes the motive may be good but it may not adopt proper means for end result which is satisfactory or opposite to the situation or demand of time. Here ethics sets a judgmental scale from best to worst.

It determines the attitudes, activities and actions in attaining right goals with limited or scarce resources through a proper processing with intellectual state of mind.

11

Ethics and its Relation to— Values, Norms and Morals

As Salmon and Hanson says, "ETHICS are a way of life. It is awareness that one is an intrinsic part of a social order, in which the interests of the others and one's own interests are inevitably intertwined."

It is defined as a set of values and principles underlined within a specific individual who recognizes or identifies him from the rest of the society.

It is the study of people's rights and duties, the moral rules that people apply in making decisions and the nature of the relationships among people.

Managerial ethics refers to the moral standards used to govern manager's behaviour and to determine right/wrong, good or evil. Ethical behaviour is the acts consistent with the moral standards or codes of conflict established by society.

Thus the above brief explanation helps us to determine that the ethics includes VALUES, MORALS and NORMS. All these when combined together forms ETHICS. All these are values, morals and norms are related to ethics.

Values

Values are the assumption – what is right, what is wrong, what is important for the society. The value represents basic convictions that a specific mode of conduct or end-state of existence is personally or socially preferable to an appropriate mode of conduct.

Values are most stable and enduring characteristics of individuals. They are the basis upon which attitudes and personal preferences are formed as well as the basis for crucial decisions.

Example of values— Controlled greed, pursuit for pleasure, truthfulness, honesty, sacrifice, compassion and charity, sacrifice, trust, cooperation etc., which all leads to the following of ethics or ethical code of conduct.

A value is one of the tools of Ethics.

A manager/employee can be said to be ethical is he/she follows certain values in their behaviour as well as in their decision making and in their actions. For example, to pay tax is business ethics which has the value of honesty/truth involved in it.

How ethics creates values:-

The ethical code of conduct have to be applied in the business practices for a continuous period of time or for perpetual period and in this way it earns long-term goodwill for the corporate culture and also for the society and the nation.

The values created by the ethical principles have life-long impact, from the viewpoint of society and is an adequate basis for ethical decision-making. The individual or businesses base their decisions on self interest alone.

It is being stated that:-

ETHICS = MORAL VALUES – SELF – INTEREST

Whenever, there are conflicts of interests one should try to settle the conflicts or solve the conflicts.

The ethics, thus, generally creates values for the entire system as a whole. This can be visible by following points:-

- Ethics have long-term cultural impact on the firm.
- Ethics bins the rational persons and drives out the unethical persons.
- As the ethics has long-term impact, the strategic benefits can be developed in the system.
- Ethics creates a different atmosphere which is ideal and unique for one to be acceptable.

- It plays a vital role by integrating the outside factors with the inside factors and brings equity to the practitioners.

Thus, the ethics of an organization at work is tied to exercising the intrinsic human values.

It is the individual values which enables firm to flourish and which enables to create its credibility, goodwill and net worth in the society. Thus, the business ethics is formed only because of the various values adopted by its managers.

In the absence of the relevant values and the corresponding ethical practices, some promoters and managers may intentionally or unintentionally, dilute the possible safeguards of laws and organizational systems and rules. A more enduring long-term foundation for corporate governance can be with through VALUES and ETHICS. The board especially the chairman and the non-executive director should demand and approve the enunciation of the core values to guide all major decisions, operations and behaviour in the company. The values may be a blend of the better values in society, that particular industry and the aspirations of the organizational members.

Examples of such values:-

- Rising levels of sense, serine to all the multiple stakeholders of the business, both external and internal.
- Vishwasatha, trusteeship of the promoters and managers.
- Dharma, fair dealings with all stakeholders, business partners and all other entities.
- Optimum karma, contribution through creation of wealth, jobs, exports, innovation etc.
- Good corporate citizenship, through legal compliance social responsibility etc.

Ethics – Morals/Common Morality

Morality is concerned with good and evil. Every human relationship is governed by two considerations: what in fact exits and what in fact ought to be. Every group prescribes for its members certain rules of conduct which ought to be observed by them. For example, the family prescribes that the child should obey his parents. The state prescribes that the politicians ought to treat their positions as a public trust. The firm prescribes that all its employees should work in cooperation. Thus, there are found certain rules of social behavior in every group which should and ought to be observed by its members. These rules and principles concerned with good and evil as manifested to conscience constitute what is called MORALITY. These rules are admitted at large by community. Honesty, faithfulness, virtue, truthfulness is some of the moral concepts. When we say that a man is morally good, we mean he is trustworthy, honest and virtuous.

Moral rules or common, morality are the core concepts and language of ethics. The morals aspects of ethics absolutely depend upon or are concerned with the business practices. It has diereses impact on the decision makers and so also the personals working in the business organization. It is the body of moral rules which governs ordinary ethical problems.

These are the rules we live by most of times.

Whenever, a business manager has to take decisions, he/she take by keeping in mind the moral rules.

So morals are principles, beliefs and practices that describe values and guides are actions.

The basic principles of common morality or the language of ethics are as follows:-

1. Promise keeping
2. Non-Malevolence
3. Mutual aid
4. Respect for persons, and
5. Respect for property

These principles have to be applied in the basic tools of the ethics-Business Ethics.

Morals are concerned with both external acts internal motives. Its violation is not punishable by the state. It is a universal concept. Morality is subjective.

Morality is concerned with what is deepest and intimate in human desire. Without moral norms human society would perish. It is a moral code which controls the individual so that he does what the group believes he should.

Whereas ethics can be defined as asset of values and principles underlined within a specific individual which recognizes or identifies him from rest of the society.

A members organization is an impossibilility.Without norms, behaviour of the employees/individuals would be unpredictable. The standards of behaviour involved in norms, give order to the social relations in the firm. The interaction or cooperation can flow smoothly, if the individuals follow the group norms, and thus maintain ethical business environment.

Norms also influence individuals' attitudes as well as his motives. Norms are specific demands to act, made by his group and are much more stable.

The individual becomes a good member to the extent he abides by the norms. The norms determine and guides the actions an individual.

If an individual/employee abides by the norms of workplace then the ethical environment could be build up and maintained.

The various norms also help to understand the ethics of a firm. These norms also reflect the values of an individual.

The business norms are enforced in order to produce ethical environment. Examples of some norms are:-

Ethics and Norms

Norms are standards of group behaviour- An essential characteristics of group life is that it is posses of a set of values which regulates the behaviour of individual members. Groups are the products of relationships among the members. When a member of individuals interacts, a set of standards develops that regulates their relationship and modes of behaviour. These norms are general standards of conduct that helps individuals judge what is right or wrong, good or bad at any firm, home etc.

Norms are enforced for various reasons are:-

- To facilitate survival of the group.
- To simplify or clarify role exceptions.
- To help group members avoid embarrassing situations.
- To express key group values and enhances the group's unique identity.

Defined in the words of Robert Kreitner, "norms are general standards of conduct for various social settings".

According to Broom and Selzmick, "The norms are the blueprints for behaviour, setting limits within which individuals may seek alternate ways to achieve their goals."

They denote expected behaviour or even ideal behaviour. They incorporate value judgments.

- Norms related to group survival.
- Norms which clarifies role exceptions.
- Norms which avoids embarrassment and protects self-image

These are certain norms which emphasis key values and enhance group's identity.

12

Teaching Ethics

Understanding the Dimension of Ethics

Ethics is a question of more formal articulation by the organized groups of a society. Professional have associations with the code of ethics while society or community as a mode of morality.

Even if the code of ethics is firmly defined by formal association of society, it's practitioner as in business and education are the actors. Ethics is not simply the laws of appropriate human conduct and relationships but are urge to do good and be good to others which ultimately fulfill it in laws. Thus ethical dimensions cannot be divorced from the moral of society and value of actors. Ethics operate between law and morality.

Thus we need to look at ethics at the intersection of these 4 following theories: Law, Morality, Self and Society.

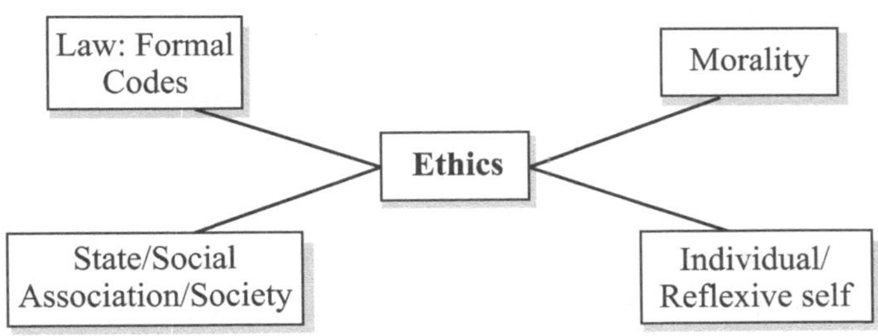

The Horizon of Business Ethics

What is Business Ethics?

Business ethics is concerned primarily with the relationship of business goals and technology to specifically human ends. It studies the impact of act of good on individual, the firm, the business community and society as a whole. Business ethics studies the special obligation which a person and a citizen accept when he or she becomes a part of the world of commerce.

Ethics refers to a process of reasoning which enables one to make better sense of "who is harmed and who is benefited by each alternative, whose rights are protected and whose violated".

Issues in teaching Business Ethics:

Through it is challenging to put business ethics into practice especially when the wider environment seems to reward unethical business practice such as bribery and nepotism, the challenge for both education and management is still to learn how to cope with these challenges.

The question of teaching anything be it ethics or electronics - involves two issues among other things, and they are:- **What to teach (which also involves questions of what is the best way of teaching a particular subject in order to function of teaching realize it's end).**

There are two modes of teaching business ethics:-

1. Principle based model
2. Virtual based model

In principle based model, principle of business ethics are explained.

In virtual based model of teaching of business ethics, the emphasis is on looking at the company as a virtue seeking - being struggling to create an ethics for itself and gain a distinct character.

Ethical issues to be taught:

A concern with ethics can help us see that in each area of business and management there is an ethical dimension which needs to be addressed.

We must know that the business corporation, like any other social environment. IT creates a moral ecology shaping countless types of teachers we must assist our students in analyzing both, deceptively and normatively the institutional ethics to the business organizations. This is one way of addressing the transferability of learning to the business context. Whether describing or prescribing, we must be able to identify ethical dimensions of corporate strategy, policy and decision making.

In the language of virtue ethics, we might say that a company implicitly or explicitly decides what kind of company it intends to be? It creates a form of character for itself and its employees and expects certain kind of behaviour to flow from such a character.

If we reemphasize the basic social values such as love, kindness, honesty, integrity, uprightness, social responsibility, etc. We would be certainly on the right track.

The question is how to regain these values on the lost paradise? The simple solution to this problem is to make ethics and values and integral part of management education.

Students need the philosophical perspective as a base to develop this thinking process and strategy for dealing with ethical issues. They also need a wide variety of cases, including executive level cases, in which to test own values and develop and understanding of the ethical dimensions of business decisions.

Importance of teaching ethics:

There is a study carried out at Harvard business school by three of its faculties. One of the researchers tells us of the response of the students to the required ethics module at H.B.S.

- One student says that earlier he didn't consider ethical issues as important ones but after taking course on ethics, he has become aware of the need to ask the question of, what is going to be the impact of this decision on the people, that live in that area and environment.
- Another student says that the difference such a course has made is in level of analysis. When you talk about whom are all people involved.
- Ethical consciousness and commitment can continue to undergo transformation atleast throughout formal education has to be the foundation of any program of teaching ethics.
- An overemphasis of SWM (Shareholders Wealth Maximization) Objectives of managers, on a misunderstanding of its true implication and theoretical foundation means that if these are misunderstood then

it can lead to dangerous or disastrous consequences for consumers, employees in the general population. So teaching ethics is extremely necessary in present scenario.

Barriers to teaching ethics:

- According to some research in the H.B school, some faculties feared that they would be asked to teach ethics as a distinct subject.
- Some faculties feared that teaching a course on ethics would bring very few professional rewards.
- Many faculties felt that integration of ethics into the class soon can threaten their self confidence who "identify strongly with their role as experts" in their professional field without giving or having the same confidence on ethics issues.
- Some teachers as well as some students felt that they need to pay some attention to ethics in their own lives before they can talk it in the classroom.
- Some faculties raised a number of teaching questions like how should a faculty respond to a student's behaviour that appears very much unethical.

PRACTICALLY APPLICABILITY

While the first course exposes students to observe the commercial enterprise as a way of considering the ethical or existing aspects of life and work. The last course is designed to provide an opportunity for students to formulate their own views about the purpose of business, the appropriate norms of business practice and strength and weakness of markets in providing for the common good.

The ethics related courses at the school can be:

1. Comparative Business – Govt. relating
2. Law and corporate management
3. Power and influence
4. Self assessment and career capitalism
5. Coming of managerial capitalism

Different surveys have been conducted in this regard. According to that students are not the problem, almost all of them are eager to talk about purpose and principle, which explore the systematic cause and consequences of unethical behaviour. They are interested to study outstanding leader and organization as they grapple with their ethical dilemmas and to identify opportunities to contribute to the larger community. The problem rest with the failure of education to encourage and assist students in their search for purpose and worth.

In today's scenario ethics are very important. There is a lot of debate among corporate commentary about **Can ethics be taught?**

There are certain arguments against teaching ethics:

People are born with certain values. It is said that ethics are in both. People cannot learn by lecturers.

- Values are cultured in homes: It is the home where a child learns the values: Home is the primary school for any person.
- Values are internal: Ethics are internal. There cannot be any external ethics.

Arguments in favour of teaching ethics:-

1. Values shaped by external environment: Values cannot be fully developed on their own. They develop in a conductive environment.
2. Value is relative: We delegate our one value with other value. It means we have to prioritize our values/ethics.

Jim Akers, Chairman of IBM Corporation wrote in 1989, "I whole heartedly favour ethical instruction".

Courses in business ethics in undergraduate and MBA program or in the business setting are essential. But these courses are no substitutes for caring and loving parents in ethics development or for a wholesome community in our school and work places.

An increasing number of schools are teaching business ethics and an increasing number of professors are doing research in this subject. An increasing number of companies are forming board committees with the title "committee on social responsibility". It's because we all are well informed about the business environment. For example, a firm might think that to increase profit, it might cut the quality of the products perhaps in little ways that management might try to improve productivity by improving harsh rules on its employees. Thus unethical behaviour is sure way to end a business career.

One of the most encouraging developments is a heightened interest in business ethics on the part of top management. Some highly placed executives are coming out from behind the corporate veil and speaking publicly on the necessity of producing goal ethics. These people are the key if the people at the top do not have.

Ethics as a Tool for Moral Training in the Organization

The ethics program is essentially useless unless all staff members are trained about what it is, how it works and their roles in it. The nature of the system may invite suspicion if not handled openly and honestly. In addition, no matter how fair and up-to-date is a set of policies; the legal system will often interpret employee behaviour (rather than written policies) as de facto policy. Therefore, all staff must be aware of and act in full accordance with policies and procedures (this is true, whether policies and procedures are for ethics programs or personnel management). This full accordance requires training about policies and procedures.

1. Orientation of new employees to the organization's ethics program during new-employee orientation.
2. Review the ethics management program in management training experiences.
3. Involving staff in review of codes is strong ethics training.
4. Involving staff in review of policies (ethics and personnel policies) is strong ethics training.
5. One of the strongest forms of ethics training is practice in resolving complex ethical dilemmas. Have staff use any of the three ethical-dilemma-resolution methods in this guidebook and apply them to any of the real-to-life ethical dilemmas also listed in this guidebook.
6. Include ethical performance as a dimension in performance appraisals.
7. The best ethics trainer: Bill Goodman, Chief Human Resource Officer at Aveda, describes, "We start our training even in our job ads, but the best trainer is the behaviour of our leaders."
8. Give all staff a copy of this free "Complete Guide to Ethics Management."

Moral and Ethical Issues – How it Modifies Business Behaviour

It is vital for a business to take moral and ethical issues into consideration when developing their corporate strategy. This is especially true for companies like Exxon and Ford, which operate on a global basis. Their actions affect the environment, etc. The manufacture of any item involves using raw materials. Cars are made primarily of steel. Steel itself is produced from pig iron, which has to be extracted from the earth. The extraction of the pig iron will cause harm to the environment, e.g. destruction of areas of natural beauty.

Manufacturing the steel, produces waste materials, which requires disposal. The manufacturing of cars also causes waste materials, which in turn have to be disposed of. The disposal of such waste materials can cause harm to the environment, e.g. pollution of rivers, the atmosphere, etc.

Using cars causes pollution. The waste materials (carbon dioxide, etc.) from using petrol are released into the atmosphere and cause such problems as the "green house" effect. External pressure groups such as Green Peace attempt to influence public awareness about the dangers from pollution caused by cars. Raising public awareness and concern puts pressure on governments to take action.

There may be several other examples in this manner. The three parties i.e. society, business people and government have to be concerned about these issue. A moral or ethical education can influence and stimulate the young generation who can be a better manager of the future.

13

Holistic Approach in Decision Making

The term Holistic refers the wholeness of any thing, any action, any concept in any discipline of management and life. It sees any thing as a whole but not as a part.

In this competitive world, when we talk of management it is a strategic approach, which works for group success against an opponent or competitors. Here, every businessman a management professional see the market as his or their own customer or prospect and every body seeks for only his survival and growth. In the same way the governments and politicians think for the development of their own state and nation. Nobody cares for others. Nobody thinks for the development of every individual, society and country. The ancient Indian thought talks of holistic approach, which advocates, the development and growth of everybody. It sees the world as a whole or one i.e. 'Vasudhaiva Kutumbkam' The holistic approach of management refers the management functioning and decision-making process in combined and united manner with no opponent but unity of all corporate members working in 'transnational way' for the good of all people.

Value Driven Holistic Management

Values express 'Dharma' or divine nature and integrity of working.

Dharma

It is the law of delivering moral obligation with right attitude for happiness of one's own life and in the life of others. It stands for all those ideals influences institutions and conduct of life and shape the character of human being as individual as well as a member of society, there are three divine elements which shapes the moral duty or dharma.

1. **Spirit:** Every human being has a soul, which is the divine element of the super power or God. It directs and oblige the mind for right work i.e. spirit. This spirit reflects in the actions of an individual. A person recognizes the spirit as the boss or the chief director of body, which declares 'Be good and Do good' in the light of consciousness.
2. **Righteousness:** It refers the right action, which is based on ethics and values of the individual as well as the society. Right action reflects in correct result, which is helpful in achieving the divine objective of life.
3. **Fearlessness:** When there is divine soul within the human being no body can touch in doing the right thing. There is a protection against fear where a person feels strong and bold the divine tough helps in converting the difficulties and threats in opportunities where success comes closer.

When we ignore the divine law of Dharma, we feel isolated and incomplete. Dharma guides and helps in conducting the right action attitude and right path for the greater success of life.

Integrity

1. **Wholeness:** It refers the unity or totality i.e. completeness.
2. **Goodness:** It refers all those essential values that make the individual perfect. These values are: honesty, kindness, truthfulness, morality etc.
3. **Self Discipline:** It refers self-control over one's own actions attitude and behaviour prevent from diverting from the right path.
4. **Inner Truth:** It is the instrument or perfection guiding the course of action in right manner achieving the objective.

5. **Courage:** It refers the confidence of an individual in doing any work and making several decisions for the right objective with right motive.

These five factors make a person motivated, confident and strong enough in conducting any course of action and decision-making process.

Why Value Drive Holistic Management?

1. **To maintain the man-machine equation:** Till 19th century man was regarded as a commodity. Gradually with the development of behavioral theories of management the human relation at work place received attention. Now we talk for human welfare and satisfaction the existence of soul and potential energy has been recognized and we are trying to achieve perfection and excellence in our actions. Value driven management recognized the divine model of man, which modifies the man-machine equation. This concept advocates the man as master of machine or technology. The result produced by the human being with the help of machine or technology.
2. **For the shake of Natural Resources:** The growth of industrialization ignores saving the natural resources. There is an exploitation of these resources for pure selfish motive, which do not care for others and for our future. Value Driven Holistic management talk of favourable and pollution free environment to assure sustainable economic development without disturbing ecological balance and cordial relationship between man and nature.

Essentials of Holistic Approach for Managers:

1. Work in unity with no opponent but one nation.
2. Employees should be respected for their innate infinite work capacity and divinity.
3. Managers should stand out no more administrator but a facilitator, a team builder, a dynamic inspire, a friend, a corporate ideal with distinct futuristic vision about the organization.
4. Manager should work with patience, calm, all loving affection, as a guide with a holistic vision and a respect to the divinity in each member of the organization.
5. All work high or low, blue colour or white colour should be respected as equally dignified avenues for manifesting one's own inner excellence, inner beauty and higher character and integrity.

The new holistic paradigm based on latest scientific experiments, have found a holistic universe where each mind is connected with every other mind and each mind is only a part of the cosmic mind.

DECISION-MAKING

Decision-making is one of the most skillful activities required by the managers. Decision-making process plays a very crucial role for the success of the individuals as well as the organization in achieving the goal and objective. It is the intellectual and intuitive approach of choosing the right alternative or course of action from a number of options or alternatives which suits most the organizational needs".

This skill requires for making the decision under a complex and ever changing environment of business. We can outline some of the skill required for decision-making.

1. Through knowledge of the subject or work.
2. Awareness about the latest development and changes.
3. Ability to choose the right idea or action required for success.
4. Effective implementation of ideas to enhance the efficiencies, and
5. Consistent performance.

Managers should make decision keeping in view the various interest group such as workers, customers, supplier etc. those decisions should be taken which do not harm society.

Self-interest of managers should not hinder a perception of problem. His aim shouldn't be personal but social welfare and his decision should be in its favour of that backward and forward linkages of decisions need to be properly understood.

Decision should leave the manager in a state of healthy mental peace. We should have a positive attitude.

Decision taken should go for common good and after taking decision we should remain calm and peaceful.

Decision creates more of unity and harmony in the environment. One should be a good listener and also try to understand others. There should be unity among employers and employees and decision should be taken in favour of everyone.

The manager should give more of himself to the task than merely taking or receiving. One should have separated his personal and professional life. Detract your personal problem and work with heart for holistic benefit.

Requisites of Good Decision:

1. The self-interest of a manager should not hinder a clear perception of problems. He is there at a position of a representative, thus, the aim should not be personnel, but social.
2. Decision should leave the manager in a state of healthy mental peace. One should always have confident in oneself and feel that the decision taken by us is good and will do good to other. If there is an attitude that the decision taken by me would calm and peaceful, therefore, such decisions need to be taken that are good to all.
3. Creation of unity and harmony. If you want to influence you first need to listen to and understand the other person, Wise executives encourage communication outside traditional lines of reporting. 'Unity is strength' If the team is united than only we can lead to success.

The Indian Ethos teaches us to awaken the infinite power in the individual by showing respect to even the lowest of workers, instead' of dictating or exploiting their ignorance. The age of nations is now over. The time has come for men to shake off their prior prejudices and turn as one man to building the nations. The problems in Indian organizations can only be solved which looked at in a new light of international grounds. Ancient Indian wisdom considered the human being as a unique living entity having self-consciousness with a complete set of mind, heart and soul with intellectual knowledge. All the human being should be considered as a whole or complete personality considering his potential energy and power to development himself in acquiring perfection in professional and personnel life, which puts the person in the movement of joy, peace and harmony. This holistic approach can develop a new standard of working life in each and every discipline where we want to excel. Developing this approach there is a special role of education, which provide both moral or intellectual training. Through proper or compulsory education, human as well as working and moral values can be nurtured which can be converted in holistic results that is equally important for each and every individual on this earth and really justify standards of humanity on our mother earth.

14

Virtue Ethics

Introduction

The word virtue has been derived from the Latin word "Virtus" meaning moral excellence of a person. A virtue is a character trait valued as being good.

Virtue ethics is an approach that deemphasises rules, consequences and particular acts and places the focus on the kind of person who is acting.

The issue is not primarily whether an intention is right, though that is important; nor is it primarily whether one is following the correct rule; nor is it primarily whether the consequences of action are good, though these factors are not irrelevant. What is primary is whether the person acting is expressing good character (moral virtues) or not.

A person's character is the totality of his character traits. The character traits can be good or bad, admirable or not. The admirable character traits or the marks of perfection in character are called VIRTUES.

Virtue ethics theories maintain that habitual development of **sound character traits** determines the ethical values of persons.

Persons with strong character have cultivated intellectual, moral, emotional and social virtues to achieve the self-discipline to do the right thing. **Character provides moral foundation for one's** actions.

Virtue ethics maintains that sound, balanced character, motivation and intention is more important than the actual conduct and its consequences.

Three major types of virtue ethics theories focus on individual, work and professional character:

(a) **Individual Character Ethic** maintains development of human traits of nobility—such as courage, moderation, justice, gratitude, sense of humour, self-discipline, reliability, benevolence, caring, sincerity, understanding and wisdom—determine value of human ethical interactions.

(b) **Work Character Ethics** maintains development of traits of work such as: competence, creativity, loyalty, pride, resourcefulness, shared work, dependability, empathy, tolerance, cooperativeness, supportiveness.

These determine ethical quality of work life.

(c) **Professional Character Ethics** maintains the credentialed expertise, licensed monopoly, self-regulation, trust, truthfulness, impartiality, independence of judgment and public service of individual in associated community.

Virtue Theory

There are 2 moralities — one for the **Individuals** and the other for **Business** — but also a common moral framework for judging both individual and corporate activities, and we can gain some guidance for business behaviour by studying and understanding morally good life.

Moral Development

In the ethical approach of Virtue Theory the moral development is of importance rather than the dependence on specific moral rules.

Virtue theory asserts that there is no common agreement in contemporary society on basic moral principles because we have lost a sense of a common cultural tradition from which the moral values springs.

People have divergent opinions regarding the development of moral values, such as:–

- Some says that moral values come from the will of God.
- Other say that morality is what makes us individually happy ('do our own thing').

- Individual rights takes precedence (over) over all other rights.
- The individual is an outmoded ideal and that the good of society be our primary goad.

Due to these divergent opinions and without a common view of a cultural tradition, these moral differences lead to the mistaken view that ethical issues cannot be decided by rational means at all, but that they are only emotional responses.

Alasdair MacIntyre, Aristotle and **Lawrence Kohlberg** have contributed in the development of virtue theory.

Alasdair MacIntrye, a contemporary advocate of virtue theory, refers to prevalent moral discussion and moral views as **emovitism** i.e., one's feelings instead of rational arguments are used to make moral decisions.

The works of **Aristotle** provides the source of the moral views, which MacIntrye defends.

According to **Aristotle**, the *values to be developed* are *best learned by studying the lives of heroic persons*. Societies where such virtues as honesty, fidelity, honor and generosity are the norm point to great individuals as models that provides guidance for individuals moral action. *Aristotle believes that the virtues are communicated in this way*. For example: to find out what courage is—examine the lives of brave persons to discover, how to act courageously.

Virtue theory also emphasises the impotence of history and literature, as they are a society's cultural memory and provides examples of admirable conduct to be copied and of abhorrent (dislike intensely) conduct to be avoided.

So in Business too, the moral values are often communicated by stories about the company's founder or its leaders who remained true to the company's moral ideals even when financial disaster loomed and the temptation was strong to sacrifice values. Various business journals talk about **Corporate Culture** which refers to the way a company does business based on the actions and the attitudes of the company's founders and continued by its current executive officers.

A major difficulty in the application of virtue ethics is the question of increasingly **Multicultural Society**. There was a commonly held cultural ideal in the Aristotle Ancient Greece, in which it was easier to understand how the homogeneous society agreed on the shared values that were communicated through deeds and exploits of cultural heroes. But the present day society is multicultural and multiracial where there are lots of challenges of the increasingly (global) dimension of business activity. It is difficult to form an idea of **what a common world culture would be like**, even if we hold the view that fundamental moral values run as constants through cultural differences.

The problems of ethical relativism views that standards of right and wrong, good and bad moral values generally are defined by a given society and therefore are not applicable universally.

Virtue theory implies a relativist position, with its emphasis on shared cultural traditions and the apparent rejection of any grounds for ethics other than a shared cultural tradition.

A shared set of values frequently communicated through tales and the recounting of heroic deeds of exemplary figures from the past has a limitation as it does not provide much guidance for thinking about ethics in novel situations. For example, what standards do we apply to leveraged buyouts, hostile takeovers, plant closings, restraints on multinational corporations, or the various issues forces on us by the complexities of an emerging global economy.

The virtue theory approach provides even less guidance than we have from other ethical theories when dealing with different cultural traditions. Matters of international business ethics are so difficult precisely because they involve the clash of cultures one differing standards of conduct. But virtue theory provides many important insight into moral decision making, but by itself seems wanting in ethical guidance.

Inspite of the technological changes of our world, human needs are virtually unchanged, and the good life remains. Aristotle had no knowledge of the intricacies of corporate existence (didn't take much interest in commercial activity), he had insights into the nature of the moral life which is referred to as the good life.

Search for well Being:

By happiness, Aristotle does not mean a passing emotional response but a state in which we are ruled by rational considerations. His word for happiness is **eudaimonia.**

Happiness is a fulfilled life, one that is lived according to reason and guided by moderation.

There are two important corollaries to Aristotle's analysis:-

First, *happiness is a quality of life that one generates throughout one's life***.** It is not something that one can say we have achieved in a few months. To seek happiness is a lifetime activity. To assess your pursuit of happiness requires that you take a long–term rather than a short-term perspective.

Second, aspect of happiness, according to him, is *that one can not seek it directly, for happiness is derived from other goads that we can seek directly.* For example, if we are to be happy, we must have enough wealth to free us from poverty and we want success in our choose work. *A circle of companions and friends contributes to one's sense of well-being.*

Friendship is also important to Aristotle. Human beings are by nature social creatures and to develop our humanness fully requires we must have meaningful relationships with other people. He believes that *one individual can find fulfillment in mutually satisfying relations, and these contributes to happiness.*

A business can have friends by having Loyal Customers, Faithful **Stockholders** and Dedicated Workers. The Japanese firm's success depends upon strong networks of suppliers and distributors called KEIRETSU in which manufactures and suppliers cooperate to produce best products at lowest cost.

Aristotle adds an important moral dimension to happiness, he defines happiness as "**activity in accord with virtue**".

In other words, one can achieve happiness – in the sense of well being- by achieving moral virtue, by being honest, loyal and through becoming interdependent human beings.

The language of Aristotle can be used to describe the GOALS and PURPOSES OF BUSINESS:–

- As eudemonia (happiness) is to individuals, the profits are to the organization. Without profits a business dies. Without profits a business cannot offer employment, make products or pay investors a return on equity.
- As individuals achieve happiness by seeking other goals, in the same way the business goal of profits can be best sought if a company first pursues such goals as enduring quality of its product, service to its customers and a commitment to ensuring a stable community and workforce.

VIRTUE AS EXCELLENCE

The key word for Aristotle is VIRTUE, but the phrase "Business Virtue" is to be thought about. We directly do not find an article in the Fortune, Forbes or Business Week praising the virtue of the CEO of a major industrial firm. Yet, the business leaders do speak of their commitment to quality and excellence and these two words are close to what Aristotle means by virtue. So, business virtues implies the commitment of the firms to quality and excellence.

The English word Virtue is an imperfect translation of a Greek word **arête**. It can mean not only moral virtue but excellence in a broader sense.

Aristotle suggests that these is an arête or **excellence** for every kind of activity – that one can seek for excellence in personal relations as well as in the business relations and both are examples of virtue.

When the business leaders talk about the need for total quality management, when a manufacturing firm claims that "quality is job one", or when a company says its trademark is the "mark of excellence", these all are references to the concept Aristotle explains in arête.

In practical terms, according to MacIntyre, "there seems to be no rational way of securing moral agreement in our culture." We are tempted to think that morality is nothing but the expression of personal preferences.

Aristotle views virtue or excellence to be of 2 types:–

One type of excellence one can learn by **training** e.g.: how to run a computer, how to do calculus etc. These types of virtues are called "**intellectual virtues**".

Other type of virtue can only be obtained through habitual behaviour and are called '**moral virtues**' and emphasises on their development by engaging in moral activities.

Aristotle says, "Men become builders by building, buildings and cricket-players by playing cricket; so we too become just by doing just acts, brave by doing brave acts."

As one develops moral habits over a lifetime, it matters a lot how one behaves as they learn what kind of person.

Morals like manners are part of the training young people, received in a society, in order to help them function well and be successful at the business of being a human being.

MORAL DISPOSITION

To Aristotle, to be moral does not mean that on occasionally performs a moral act; even immoral persons do moral things sometimes, but we would call such a person moral because of an occasional good deed. A truly moral person is one who has developed a *moral disposition through the development of right habits* and *whose behaviour is consistently moral.*

This Aristotelian point is summed up by a contemporary writer C.S. Lewis, who points to the difference between doing something that is just or temperate person. He says a person who preserves in doing just actions gets in the end a certain quality of character. Now it is that quality rather than the particular actions which we mean when we talk of virtue.

An important feature of society that emphasises virtue is that its values are conveyed through **storytelling**.

A value oriented society transmits its values through the telling and retelling of the deeds of the heroes of that cultural tradition.

The goal of moral instruction is to develop the character traits similar to those of outstanding individuals, to model one's behaviour after the examples of **courage, fortitude honesty, integrity** and **loyalty** of the tradition's cultural heroes, (e.g. Once Abraham Lincoln while working as a shopkeeper's assistant, he walked several miles after work to return a few pennies to a woman he had overcharged unintentionally).

Such stories provides models for developing behaviour, that is considered ethically upstanding.

In the contemporary society this storytelling feature has been taken over by popular culture media-films, television, mass market function, lap lyrics – and the values they exhibit, have more influence on the developing attitude of young people than all the ethics classes offered in all the schools in the country.

Business – If the society's popular culture presents business leaders as rapacious and business activity as opposing the public good, then the message transmitted to young people it that business is not an ethical activity and that to be successful in business demands following of our ordinary standards of conduct.

If the company's corporate culture is filled with stories of predatory business practices and legal but not necessarily moral activities, the message to employees is clear : do anything you have to do, cut any corners possible, to advance the company's interest.

Intrinsic and Instrumental Goods

Another feature of Aristotle's analysis of ethics is the important distinction b/w intrinsic and instrumental goods.

An **intrinsic good** is something that is good in itself like health. We seek health not just because it is good for something else but because it is something we desire for its own sake. Good health helps to do many things as we can hold a job, go to schools etc. We value health for its own sake as an **intrinsic good**. Good health requires **regular exercise** or other aids to maintain our health. These activities are called **instrumental goods** which contribute to our well-being by encouraging good health.

However, what is an instrumental good in one context can become intrinsic good in another. Each one of us may have different activities that bring **happiness** and Aristotle believes that "happiness is chief and intrinsic good," for the sake of which we do all these other things.

Another important aspect of Aristotle's views on happiness is that it is a goal reached by long-term behaviours, not short-term activity, as opposed to views of contemporary writers of immediacy of reward.

If applied to Business Context, the business's intrinsic goal like happiness is the long-term profitability.

Moral Development Stages :

Although Aristotle was convinced that people develop their moral character over time and through habituatio**n** but he did not describe how this happens.

In this context, a description information is provided by Harward psychologist Lawrence Kohlberg.

Kohlberg's research centered on describing the stages of moral development and various stages through which individuals pass they mature in their moral judgment.

He divides moral development into 3 stages:–

I. Preconventional

II. Conventional

III. Post-conventional

Each one of these has 2 levels giving a total of 6 possible stages of moral development.

The Preconventional level is the one of Punishment and Reward.

The Conventional level is the one in which we seek approval of others submit to authority.

The post-conventional level is the highest level of moral development in which people seek the general welfare and act according to universal moral principles.

Kohlberg made **several conclusions** about moral development:–

- He found that people move forward, never backwards through these stages (except in cases of extreme).
- Also, individuals do not skip stages i.e., they do not do directly go from, the preconventional to post-conventional for example – persons at one level can correctly classify statements representing lower levels but not those referring to higher levels of moral development.
- Moral development is not co-related with intelligence.

15

Utilitarian Theory

'The end justifies the means', is an old saying. The ends of an action are the consequences to be obtained; the means are the actions that produce the desired results. In the extreme form the statement claims that the consequences are the only important thing, if the end to be achieved is good then anything necessary to achieve that end is good also.

Even lying, cheating, stealing and killing would be considered ethically acceptable so long as the end to be achieved is good.

It has been argued that the consequences of an action are ethically significant, that all the best motives in the world are of no value unless a moral result is achieved.

Views that claim that consequences are important for assessing the moral worth of an action are called 'Consequentialist' view, as they emphasise consequences. There are a variety of consequentialist views and one of the views as 'Utilitarianism' and its business applications in the form of cost-benefit analysis.

UTILITARIANISM

Utilitariam Theory

Utilitarianism is the name given to an ethical theory formulated in 19th century by Thinkess as **Jeremy Bentham** (1784-1832), **James Mill** (1773-1836) and **John Stuart Mill** (1806-1873).

This approach places the moral worth of an action in the action's consequences and emphasises the good of the total society, not the benefits accruing to a single individual or even a group of individuals. The Utilitarians sought to provide legislators with a clear and scientific method for evaluating legislative options.

According to Utilitarian Bentham the formula says, "One can add up all the positive aspects of a decision, contrast them with all the negative aspects and then make the decision on the grounds of producing the greatest happiness for the greatest number of people."

For Bentham the matter is simple:–

"**Pain is Bad, Pleasure is Good**," If an action produces a sum total of more pain than pleasure (for the greatest number of people) then the only consequence to be considered is the action's tendency to produce pleasure and avoid pain.

As developed by Mill and Bentham, utilitarianism aims not for the pleasure of the individual but the "greatest good for the greatest number" of people.

TYPES OF UTILITARIANISM

Two types of Utilitarianism:

I. Act Utilitarianism

II. Rule Utilitarianism

I. Act Utilitarianism

According to this, an *act is morally right if and only if it maximizes utility of an action.* This means, out of the alternative actions available to a person the action which has maximum benefits as compared to harms is the best moral action. The benefits and harms are calculated for every person who is going to be affected by the proposed action.

In the determination of which act is right, as Act utilitarian will:–

1. Set out all relevant alternative acts those are open to him;
2. **List** all the individuals who will be affected by the alternative courses of action including oneself if affected;
3. **Assess** how the individuals will be affected by the alter native acts;
4. **Compute** balance of benefit to harm for each individual affected by each act;
5. **Add** balance of benefit to harm for every affected individual;
6. **Chose** that act which has maximum utility, i.e, maximum balance of net benefits.

II. Rule Utilitarianism

Rule utilitarianism emerged as a way to overcome the shortcomings of Act utilitarianism.

Rule utilitarianism is a concept, according to which, an act is morally right only when it conforms to the rule which maximises utility for everyone.

When faced with a decision as to which act is right in particular situation, one simply needs to refer to the rule which maximises utility in the given circumstances. The act which is supported by this rule is the moral act.

For example, 'Stealing is wrong' for maximization of good of everyone, we would follow this rule while making ethical decision regarding stealing or not stealing anything.

The important distinction b/w Act Utilitarianism and Rule Utilitarianism is that the:–

Act Utilitarianism 'tends to judge each act in isolation.'

Rule Utilitarianism 'judges an act in light of a rule which takes into account collective interests of all in all circumstances.'

The Act Utilitarianism asks, "How much pleasure or pain would result if **I** did this now?"

The Rule Utilitarians asks, "How much pleasure or pain would result if **everyone** were to do this?"

Arguments Favouring Utilitarianism

1. Utilitarianism represents the ideal of co-existence in a society :

We living in a society are supposed to work towards common good to maximize well being of the society as a whole. By considering consequence of our actions on society and striving to maximize good consequences, we are able to do what is expected of us.

2. Utilitarianism is impartial and plays no favourites :

By following the principle of maximization of total utility or total good (net of bad consequences), utilitarianism leaves no room for partiality. It treats everybody as equal.

3. It forms the rational basis of decision where community interests are involved:

When decisions are to be taken at organizational or state level, the best approach to make decision is to base the decisions on consequences. For example, which preparing budgetary policy, the state would opt for those policies which would be able to produce good consequences for the nation as a whole.

4. Utilitarian theories take note of situational context :

To assess the consequences, it is essential to take the situational factors into account, as taken by utilitarian theory.

5. Utilitarianism follows the cause and effect reasoning like science :

Any decision can be proven right or wrong based on empirical searving.

6. Utilitarianism has been highly influential in economics :

Utilitarianism is the basis of many economic techniques like **Cost-Benefit Analysis**.

7. Utilitarianism is trans-cultural :

As all living being experience pain and pleasure, so the principles consider every being of diverse culture.

Criticism

1 Critics of utilitarianism have charged that it is not a total approach to the ethical decision making, as by concentrating on the consequences of actions it ignores intentions and motives, which are also important in the moral decision-making.

2. The limits can also be seen in a business content in the concept of cost-benefit analysis, a process in which the monetary costs of a certain course of action are weighed against the benefits to be gained in contrast to other possible actions.

3. It also faces limitations in its *inability on the grounds of greatest happiness principle* – to deal adequately with the rights of individuals and minority groups. For example, if the greatest happiness of the greatest number of people can be secured by denying rights to small groups, then the utilitarian principle would be unethical.

4. Utilitarians insists on *pleasure as the measure of good life*; Aristotle argues for *happiness as happiness is the goal of life.* He describes that happiness describes a much longer frame than does pleasure.

5. Another difference is that **Bentham** emphasizes only **quantitative measures**, whereas **Aristotle's** pursuit of happiness involves qualitative measures.

6. There is another difficulty in the approach :

   "Pain is bad, pleasure is good", i.e., *how does one measure pleasure*?

7. Some utilitarians as John Stuart Mill said that there is an important difference in the quality of various pleasures e.g., enjoying a movie at cinema hall or at home. Mill argues that the pleasures of the mind are superior to those of the physical side of nature of an individual.

8. Mill argues that no amount of general good for society would justify **infringements of personal liberty** or the **restriction of women's right**.

9. It also **ignores** the **rights of the minority populations** which is unethical. Greatest good can not be enhanced by ignoring rights of minority or by breaking any laws.

10. One can not use utilitarian principles on a case-by-case basis as it would take enormous amount of time.

It should be used to develop and defend rules that will bring about the best consequences for society in the long-run.

Consequences are difficult to predict:

As the situation involved more people and alternatives, it becomes more difficult to determine which action would produce the best consequences. There is no way for a person to ever know that the actually chose the 'best alternative'.

Conclusion

Thus, the utilitarian ethics had following principles:

1. **Greatest good for greatest number:** which propounds that the concept of selfishness should not be there.
2. **Emphasis on consequences and outcomes:** which means that the probable outcomes or reactions of one's actions should be acknowledged or taken into consideration.
3. **Cost-benefit analysis:** Each and every ethical duties should be confirmed by means of a comparing analysis of the ethical costs and benefits.

16

Utilitarianism and its Application to Business

There are several ways that utilitarian thinking enters into business decisions, which can be examined or studied under 2 heads:

I. Cost-Benefit Analysis.

II. Utilitarian Analysis and Defence of Free Market

I. Cost-Benefit Analysis

The application of consequentialist modes of thinking as **Cost-Benefit Analysis**: The Cost-Benefit Analysis is an accepted technique for decision-making in the business. The business cannot function effectively without such a decision procedure. The calculations of the costs of a decision and the benefit of that decision expressed is monetary terms is at the heart of utilitarian thought:

Cost-Benefit Analysis is utilitarian in 3 ways :

(a) It is consequentialist in its orientation, *directed towards a desired outcome*.

(b) It is *concerned with producing maximum benefits*.

A decision analyst using costs and benefits may not use the language of utilitarianism (greatest good for the greatest number), but clearly the company is interested in maximising sales to the greatest number of people possible and providing them the best product at the price that bring them into the market place.

(c) Like the practice of some utilitarians the costs and benefits are expressed in quantitative terms usually Rupees and Dollars.

The Cost-Benefit Analysis will not factor into the equation many qualitative considerations at all, so the cost-benefit analysis is more like the Bentham's utilitarianism.

However, the limitations to consequentialist ways of thinking as applied in the context of business.

Uncertainty of Outcomes

All the business decisions face the uncertainty of outcomes : For example, will the product be successful as indicated by various tests? Will the efforts to add to the company's product line make the company more productive? Will moving a manufacturing facility to a new location and building a more modern facility produce the desired increase in profitability and efficiency? etc.

Ethical choices in business would be easy if one could be assured that he would make only safe products, that he (firm) would pursue only those policies that increase profits and protects the jobs of workers, or would always know how much to invest in new product and process development as to overcome competition.

Because of these reasons, according to the Rule Utilitarians one should be guided by broad, general principles rather than a case-by-case cost benefit analysis.

If the businessmen knew of the outcomes of their actions, then the ethical decisions would not be as difficult as they usually are.

Several current business practices are controversial because it is not known whether they are beneficial or harmful to society. As certain hostile takeovers. Like Sir James Goldsmith, a British businessman who has attempted several takeovers in the U.S., argues that he serves as a kind of cleansing agent, clearing up inefficiency and waste and making companies more profitable than they were before.

The result is a more productive and competitive company, one that is better able to survive in an increasingly worldwide marketplace.

However, certain critics of such take overs argue that takeovers focus only on short-term gains, not long-term productivity they also destroy productive companies in the name of individual greed, and they cause unemployment for displaced workers and contribute to community economic decline.

The Role of Compromise

It is also the case that many business decisions, and certainly most engineering decisions, are the result of a series of compromises. For example, it is possible for engineers to design an automobile that would be much safer than those currently available.

However, the design requirements and the costs of an automobile that was built to be as safe as is technically possible.

First, it would be well protected against collision, even against larger vehicles such as trucks, making the car extremely heavy and therefore, requires a larger engine, which would burn more fuel. To make the car more reliable would require minute and extensive testing, as done for airframes and engines. Then, everything about the auto would be expensive – from the larger tyres required to support the extra weight to the additional thicker window glass and so on.

Seeking over greater margins of safety, the company would be forced to price the automobile out of the reach of most purchasers.

No company could afford to mass-produce such a product and automobile ownership would be restricted to the wealthy few. Because of the limited number of automobiles, there would be little spending on roads and highways, inadequate incentives for oil companies to search fuel supplies, and limited facilities to repair and maintain vehicles.

To bring automobile ownership to a majority of people (the greatest good for the greatest number), manufacturer seek to make the best products for the lowest cost so that they will enjoy the largest market and produce greatest profit to the companies. This is cost-benefits analysis at work, and without it modern economics would be impossible.

Protecting Individuals

Various business decisions are caught in a tension between the obvious desirability for a company to produce an absolutely safe product and the need to make the product available to the widest possible market at the lowest possible cost. This tension can not be easily resolved. If it is resolved in favour of absolute safety of a product then it would produce disaster for a business enterprise either the company's products will not find a niche in the marketplace, with major consequences to the company; or its products will cause injury or death to the users resulting in losses to the company in the form of damage and litigation cost.

However, the company cannot trade off (rule out) individual safety as against corporate profits. So, the cost-benefit analysis cannot ignore the rights of individuals in an unrestrained way.

II. Utilitarian Defenses of the Free Market

Free Market

It is the mechanism in which the players of the market have extensive control over the market. The individual players decides the destiny of the market without accepting the challenges of the regulatory authorities like control over the efficacy of market factors. As a result, the price determination, product distributions and other supply or acquisition factors are playing with the hands of marketplayers.

The marketplayers or operators are the guide, philosophers and the utilities of the entire market forces. Hence, it is the market in which 100% autonomy is granted to the elements interacting the market.

The consequentialist considerations, in their utilitarian norms, can provide a powerful way of thinking about the business activity and this could also be found in the *defense of the free market.*

The free market approach to national economic policy is being organized for a principal reason – free market economies are the most productive, and means that more people benefit than under any other economic scheme. The free market creates a greater totality of wealth i.e. available for distribution to a greater number of people.

In a free market economy more people will have more goods and services and be able to participate more fully in the economic life of the society.

As implied to business practices this implies that companies must honour the freedom of marketplace and any attempt by a company to manipulate the market so as to reduce this freedom is unethical.

Example price fixing, collusion to restrict the supply of goods and services, and other anti-competitive practices.

Just as the utilitarian theory needs to be supplemented by concern for individual rights, so a free market economy requires something more than the forces of supply and demand to provide for those individuals who are not benefited by the free market: workers who loose their jobs due to market forces, those who lack the shills find their niche in the market, or those the market rejects as too old, too sick or too poorly educated. These functions are usually assigned to government; but how much the government should intrude into the marketplace and the form of that intrusion should relate to social policy matters.

However, with all these imperfections, the market does seem to be the best way of organizing society's productive capacities to provide the greatest good for the greatest number of people.

Part - IV

Business Ethics

- Meaning, Nature, Scope of Business Ethics
- Relevance of Business Ethics
- The Changing Workplace
- Ethical Issues in Marketing
- Whistle-Blowing
- Ethical Responsibilities of Business Towards Consumers and Employees
- Employee Discrimination

17

Meaning, Nature, Scope of Business Ethics

Doing business ethically means holding right things right and wrong things wrong in business. For example, if a product of certain quality has been promised to a customer, he should deliver the promised quality; if certain emoluments have been promised to an employee, he should be given those emolument, no harm should be caused by the business to any human being or society or to the environment.

The term **business ethics** simply refers to ethics as it applies to business.

Just as Political Ethics is concerned with the ethics of political affairs, **Accounting Ethics** are concerned with the fair accounting practices, **Business Ethics** are concerned with the **moral issues in business.**

Frederick and Lawrence define business ethics as "application of general ethical ideas to business".

It applies reasoning to business situations and activities, it is an attempt to resolve or atleast classify those moral issues that arise in business.

Business Ethics are centrally concerned with the business conduct. A conduct of the business may be ethical or unethical.

If a business delivers lesser quantity to the customer than promised, it is an unethical conduct, if a business supply quality goods to customers, it is an ethical conduct.

Business ethics provides essential support for maximizing long-term owner value of the business.

There is a need to emphasise the ethical conduct of business because over the period of time, business values have been deteriorated drastically.

In the effort to earn more and more profits, businesses do compromise on the issue of ethics. They adopt such unethical practices as obtained finances using wrong or misleading financial information; exploiting employees by paying low wages; providing sub-standard good, not keeping promises, using unfair meeats to gain business advantage, etc.

Thus, there is a strong need to reinforce ethical conduct in the businesses.

NATURE OF BUSINESS ETHICS

Any business, if it wants to survive and grow in the long-run must strike a balance between its social obligations and economic objectives.

Most businesses encounter 2 types of ethical problems: -

1. **Overt Ethical Problems:** Overt ethical problems deals with bribery, theft, collusion etc. they are transparent and reprehensible.
2. **Covert Ethical Problems:** Covert ethical problem occur in *corporate acquisitions, marketing and personnel policies, capital investments* etc.

They are complex, clear and deft ethical solution.

An ideal ethical decision comprises of fellow Virtues :

1. Right – Morally Correct
2. Equitable – Just and equal
3. Good – Highest good for all concerned
4. Proper – Appropriate and acceptable
5. Fair – Honesty
6. Just – Action

The concept of ethics, therefore, is very **vague, abstract** and **unstructured.**

There is no universally accepted definition of ethics because ethics is dependent on moral standards.

Moral standards are dependent on a value system, and value systems are dependent on a value system, and value systems are dependent on individual's background. The background of each individual differs according to his a her experience. Hence, the ethical practices of people are different.

Scope

Since Business Ethics is the normative science of conduct i.e., its function is to judge the moral worth of conduct with reference to a norm ideal or standard the scope of business ethics is wide.

Business Ethics covers all aspects of business as there is no business conduct which is totally free from moral considerations.

As a science of conduct, it is concerned with the ideal or standard to which business conduct should conform.

Thus, it enquires into the nature of springs of action or impetus, the forces that impels businessman to action, motives, intentions, nature of voluntary or involuntary actions etc.

It lays down the ideal of highest good and judges our conduct in the right of that ideal.

Ethical issues are everywhere, at all levels of business activity.

Business ethics concern the ground rules of individual company and societal behaviour.

The scope of Business Ethics covers the following key levels:-

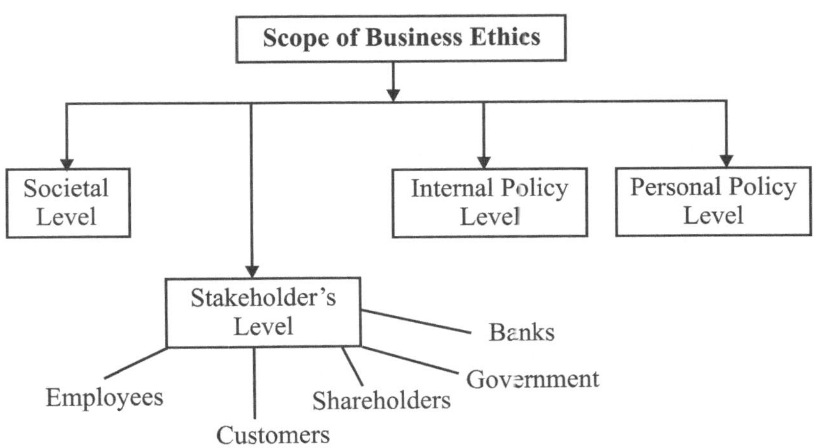

A. Societal Level

- Concern for poor and down-trodden
- No discrimination against any particular section / group
- Concern for clean environment
- Preservation of scarce resources for prosperity
- Contributing to better quality of life.

B. Stakeholder's Level

The term stakeholder is a broad term which includes:

(a) Employees

(b) Customers

(c) Shareholders

(d) Banks and other lending institutions

(e) Government

a. Employees

- Security of job
- Better working conditions
- Better recommendations
- Participative management
- Welfare facilities

b. Customers

- Better quality of goods
- Goods and services at reasonably price
- Not to corner stocks and create securities
- Not to practice discriminatory pricing
- Not to make false claims about products in advertisements

c. Shareholders

- Ensure capital appreciation
- Ensure steady and regular dividends
- Disclose all relevant information
- Protect minority shareholder's interests
- Protect interests in times of mergers, takeovers and amalgamations

d. Banks and other Lending Institutions

- Guarantee safety of borrowed funds
- Prompt repayment of loans

e. Government

- Complying with rules and regulations
- Honesty in paying taxes and other dues
- Activity as partner in the progress of the country

C. Internal Policy Level

- Fair practices relating to recruitment, compensation, layoffs, perks, promotion etc.
- Transformational leadership to motivate employees to aim at better and higher things in life.
- Better communication at all level.

D. Personal Policy Level

- Not to misuse other for personal ends.
- Not to indulge in politics to gain power.
- Not to spoil promotional chances of others.
- Not to use office car, stationary and other facilities in personal use.
- Promise keeping
- Mutual help
- Not to adopt shortcuts for easy money making.
- No violence, i.e., preventing or not causing physical.
- Respect for persons and property.

18

Relevance of Business Ethics

INTRODUCTION

Ethics refers to a system of moral principles – a sense of right and wrong and goodness and badness of actions and their motives and consequences.

Business ethics refers to the application of ethics to the business. To be more specific, business ethics is the study of good and evil, right and wrong, just and unjust actions of businessmen.

To be considered ethical, businessmen must draw their ideas about what is desirable behaviour from the same sources as anybody else. Businessmen should not try to evolve their own principles to justify what is right and wrong.

Business ethics does not differ from generally accepted norm of good or bad. If dishonesty is considered to be unethical and immoral in society, then any businessman who is dishonest with employees, customers, shareholders or competitions is acting unethically and immorally.

Need for Ethics in Business

Ethical considerations are as important in management as in any ether occupation. On field of morality, personal life is not separate from business life. The social dimensions of business ethics cannot be overlooked because many problems arise from the relationship of business to the boarder society. Ethical considerations are significant for managers due to the following reasons:

(i) For every individual job is the centre of life unless job values are in harmony with the rest of life, he cannot be a happy and healthy person.

(ii) Modern society is an industrial society. Therefore business values becauses the values of the society as a whole.

(iii) A business executive must take into consideration the moral and social considerations because these are the real motivating factors.

(iv) When an organisation fails to behave in accordance with the social expectations, it may lose not only its image and market share but its very right to exist.

Factors Governing Business Ethics

Business Ethics has deep and wide roots in society some of the pressure points of ethical behaviour are given below:

(i) Value Forming Institutions

The value system of an individual is shaped by various institutions, eg., family, religion, school and the govt. These institutions prescribe what is good or bad for an individual. Right behaviour is rewarded while wrong behaviour is punished. The values fostered by one institutions are reinforced by others.

(ii) Organizational Goals

The objectives of an organization influence the value of its members. A business is an economic institution and it must be profitable. Many limes, managers may be forced to compromise their personal ethical value ethics in order to achieve organizational goals. But the goal may be tempered by many values. Leadership, integrity, knowledge and skills, survival are some of them.

(iii) Work and Career

Work refers to the job/task/responsibilies while career represents a series of jobs / position. Each work has its own values and persons performing the work follow these values.

(iv) Superiors

Most people succumb to pressure from superiors in doing things that they may consider unethical otherwise.

(v) Peers and Colleagues

An individual in a work group tends to conform to the norms of the group. He does so either to get approval or friendship of his colleagues. He adopt the attitudes, beliefs and values of the group to which he is associated.

(vi) Professional Codes

These days two types of lodes are available :

- Big companies formulate their philosophy or weed to guide the behaviour of their employees. The main objective of these documents is to build the company's image by showing the company's concern for ethical behaviour in the society.
- Company policies contain a code of conduct to guide actions that have an ethical conduct etc. AIMA.

Business Ethics are Important?

(i) Ethics corresponds to basic human needs

It is a human trait that human desires to be ethical, not only in his private life but also in his business affairs where, being a manager, he know his decisions may affect the lives of thousand of employees. However, most people want to be part of an organization which they can respect and be publicly proud of, because they perceive its purpose and activities to be honest so beneficial to the society.

(ii) Value create credibility with the public

A company perceived by the public to be ethically and socially responsive will be honoured and respected even by those who have no intimate knowledge of its actual working. There will be an instinctive prejudice in favour of its products, since people believe that the company offers value for money.

(iii) Value give management credibility with employees

Values are supposed to be a common language to bring leaderships and its people together. The management has credibility with its employees precisely because it has credibility with the public. Weather sound business strategy, nor a generous compensation policy and fringe benefits can win employee credibility and and perceived moral and social uprightness can.

(iv) Values help better decision making

An ethical attitude helps the management make better decisions i.e., decisions which are in the interest of the public, their employees and the company own long-term good, even though decision making is slower. This is so becomes respect for ethics will force a management to take various aspects-economy social and ethical in decision making.

(v) Ethics and profit

Ethics and profit go together. A company which is inspired by ethical conduct is also profitable one. Value driven companies are sure to be successful in the long run, though in the short run, they may lose money.

(vi) Law cannot protect society, ethics can

Ethics are important because the govt., law and low yes cannot do everything to protect society. Technology develops of aster than the govt. can regulate. People in an industry after know the dangers in a particular technology better than the regulatory agencies. Further govt. cannot always regulate all activities which are harmful to society. Where law fails, ethics can succeed. An ethical oriented management takes measures to prevent pollution and protect workers' health even before being mandated by law.

Benefits of Business Ethics

(i) To Managers

- Knowledge of business ethics will help managers in resolving ethical issues/dilemmas as they arise.
- Knowledge will help managers in setting highly responsible tone for the organization – in individual judgements and decisions whether ethical or not.
- The study of business ethics will provide conscentious managers with morally responsible approach to the business.
- It helps managers to realize their social responsibility and creates awareness of social and moral values.
- The study of business ethics inculcates high level of integrity in managers.

(ii) To Organization

- Promote a strong public image.
- Attention to business ethics has substantially improved society.
- Maintain a moral course in turbulent times.
- Cultivate strong teamwork and productivity.
- Support employee growth and meaning.
- Builds openness, integrity and strong teams in the workplace.

Conclusion

In nutshell, business ethics provides a basic outlook. "The Essence of Business Ethics" cautions against one erroneous expectation. People with immoral habits will not change by receiving a book on business ethics.

It has to be realized that business ethics connot do without ethics. Sound ethics pay off in the long-run. Much neglect of ethics occurs out of incompetence, cowardice myopia.

Ethical values, consistently applied, are the cornerstones in building a commercially successful and socially responsible business.

19

The Changing Workplace

Many changes have occurred in the workplace over the years as employees and employers have developed new relationships that reflect changing interests and concerns.

The changes have taken place in relation to the place of work in people's lives and the way in which they understand this activity.

These changes are basic to people's attitude toward work and the workplace and are reflected in the policies of private and public institutions.

The changes involved the rise of labour unions to look after the interests of employees. These changes also relate to the changes in the contact between employees and employers.

We can summarize the changes in the workplace culture as follows:

I. The Changing Nature of Work

The notion of what work means and how work is defined has undergone major changes throughout history.

To the **ancient Greek**, work was a curse to be avoided if at all possible. They saw "work as a punishment for sin."

During the Renaissance, however, the work began to be viewed more positively. Craftsmanship and technical processes become more gratifying and intrinsically meaningful.

During the Industrial Revolution the work become the most important activity in a person's life, it was considered as a vocation that demands one's best efforts and dedication. In this phase, it was observed that by working hard, a person was supposed to be able to overcome every obstacle that life presents. Success was directly linked to one's own efforts and the material wealth a person accumulated was a measure of how much effort he or she expended. It was believed that wealth should be wisely invested and not foolishly spent on personal consumption.

As the industrial societies advanced the technology eliminated the hardest and physically demanding kinds of jobs.

With the growth of large corporate organizations, ORGANIZATIONAL ETHICS began to evolve. One of the major proposition of the organizational ethic included a belief in the group as a source of creativity and a belief in belongingness as the ultimate need of the individual. It became more important for the individual to integrate well with his or her peers in the organizations. The organizational ethics created important values applicable at workplace such as conformity at work and cooperation among working members. Dependence became a major virtue to be extolled and independent person became the social isolate who failed to integrate successfully with the group.

Work carries meaning as it affects the group or the organization and group or organizational effort is valued rather than individual effort.

Gradually with the emergence of affluent society, the nature of work changed more. The fewer hours one can spend working and the more leisure time available, the better, was the new trend.

The traditional understanding of work was replaced by the humanistic understanding of work. It implied on making work meaningful and fulfilling for the individuals. According to this work ethic, the workplace can be organized to allow for human growth and development. The focus is on self rather than on the work itself, the group or organization in which one functions or on the leisure activities one pursues.

However with all these changes, certain priorities need to be kept in mind:

- Work is to be taken seriously as the way in which people discover themselves and fulfill themselves as human beings.
- Technology and workplace must be redesigned to serve people's needs for growth and development.
- The organization is necessary to provide the setting in which people work, but it is not on end in itself.
- Hardwork is not valued for its own sake but valued in terms of what it contributes to personal development.
- Leisure is acceptable, but not as a replacement for the fulfillment that work can provide.

All these understandings of work and its place in life are being challenged by current changes in the workplace. Due to global competition and rapidly developing technology change has become inevitable.

Lifetime Employment is becoming a thing of the past and Job Security is a major concern for workers.

Terms like mobility, empowerment, teams, virtual offices, telecommuting, reengineering, restructuring, delayering, outsourcing and contingency are new buzzwords.

Companies have downsized by laying off many workers and eliminating layers of middle management.

Firms have restructured by forming teams and empowering these teams with authority to get the work done.

Outsourcing of employees have led to escape paying benefits to the full-time employees.

Many offices are virtually empty as the employees spend much time working in the field.

All these developments have led to the *redefinition of the way we work.*

Instead of lifelong employment, the emphasis is on **lifelong employability**.

The employers have an obligation to provide opportunity for self-improvement, while the employees have to take charge of their own careers and can no longer rely on a secure place in the organization. Employees are expected to share responsibility for their employment and are gaining greater control over what they do in the workplace.

The demand for professional, managerial and technical skills that pay high wages is to **increase** while the demand for crafts jobs and those of operators and laborers is expected to decrease.

Those who know how to process information and make decisions will be in demand.

All these changes are weakening and even breaking the traditional bonds between employees and among employees themselves.

The non-material rewards that come from collegiality and commonality of interests are diminishing.

The intangible values that come from work a sense of community, the shared goals of employees and employers, the exchange of ideas in the workplace and a sense of achievement and disappearing.

II. The Family Friendly Corporation

One of the newly emerging right in the workplace involves the relation of the corporation to the family.

A family-friendly corporation can be defined as on organization that acts on its responsibilities to provide employees with the means to manage the conflicting demands between work and family.

Creating a family-friendly workplace involves recognition of a responsibility to help employees meet the needs of their families, development and implementation of strategies to help employees meet the conflicting demands.

There are many types of programs that companies have adopted in some form to help employees take care of family needs for e.g.:

Flexitime where employees can work the same number of hours but determine their starting and stopping times with a range of parameters.

Part-time work or job sharing is another program or strategy that can help parents meet family needs. **Job sharing** involves two people doing essentially the same job so that each one gets some time off during the week.

The provision of **on-site or near-site day care centers** is another useful strategy for the working parents. If the day care centers are of high quality, then the parents would be secured that their children are getting good care.

Providing **time-off** when employees need is another strategy that can work effectively. This strategy help employees take time-off when a child is sick or when an aged parent needs some special attention, but this privilege must not be misused.

Using **Compressed Work Schedules** that involves giving workers a choice over the length of their work week. Instead of working the traditional five 8-hour days, employees can choose to work four 10-hour days or may be there 12-hour days. In this way they can spend more time with their families.

Thus, the above family-friendly strategies can help employees resolve the conflict between work and family.

III. The Changing Social Contract

The changes in the nature of work and in the role of labour unions have resulted in changes in the contract between employees and the corporation.

The old contract held that employees had obligation related to satisfactory attendance at work, acceptable levels of effort and performance and loyalty to corporation and management. In return to these commitment, the employees provided fair pay and fringe benefits, the chance for advancement based on seniority and merit, and some degree of job security.

As job security has evaporated because of restructuring, downsizing, and other changes in the workplace so prospects for advancement and predictable wage and benefit increases.

The management demands for individual commitment and responsibility have largely taken their place.

Changes have affected worker's morale and attitude towards jobs and the company.

Pollster Daniel Yankelovich has identified 5 patterns of employee response to the changing workplace:

1. Employees no longer believe that their job is for life.
2. They no longer believe in employer loyalty and concern.
3. They are losing confidence that they will be rewarded for learning and expanding their skills.
4. They are beginning to equate the corporate emphasis on quality with downsizing.
5. Work has become a less reliable source of satisfaction and of rewards other than money.

For a new system of work organization the following 5 principles are suggested:

1. Rejection of the traditional dichotomy between thinking and doing, conception and execution. The process requires a fundamental redistribution of decision-making authority from management to teams of workers. The workers must also be given the opportunity to develop and refine analytic and problem-solving skills.
2. Jobs that are redesigned to include a greater variety of skills and tasks and greater responsibility for the ultimate output of the organization. Workers should be free to do right thing, rather than being compelled to do the prescribed thing.
3. Substitution of a flatter management structure for the traditional, multi-layered hierarchy. The aim is to enable workers to be self-managers who are responsible for their own performance.
4. A decision-making role at all levels of the enterprise for workers, through their unions. Strategic decisions are to be jointly made by workers—acting through their unions and other stakeholders.
5. Rewards realized from transforming the work organization should be distributed on equitable terms agreed upon through negotiations between labour and management. That means a negotiated agreement to protect income and employment security to the maximum possible extent.

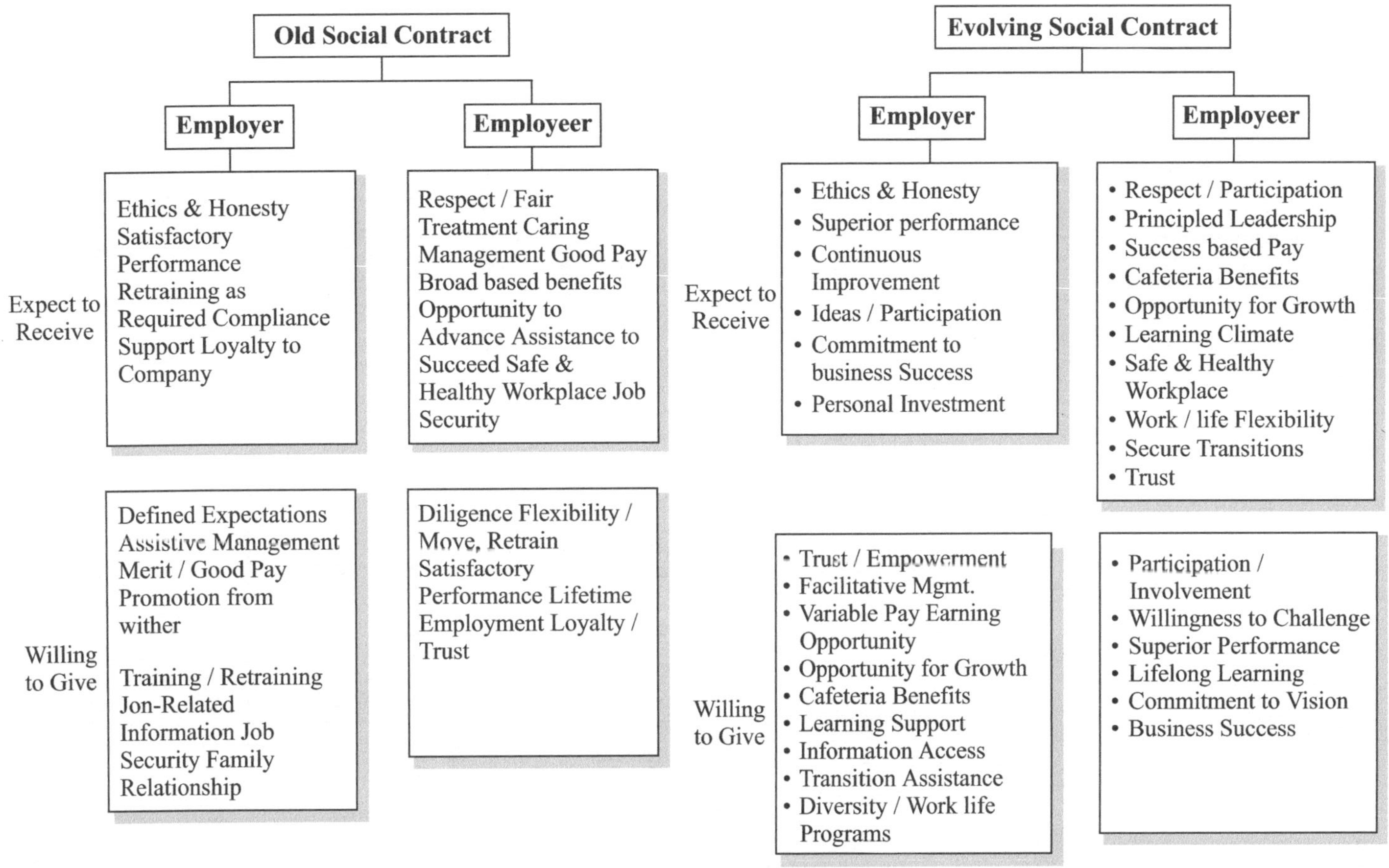
Old Social Contract
Employer
Employeer
Expect to Receive
Ethics & Honesty
Satisfactory
Performance
Retraining as
Required Compliance
Support Loyalty to
Company
Respect / Fair
Treatment Caring
Management Good Pay
Broad based benefits
Opportunity to
Advance Assistance to
Succeed Safe &
Healthy Workplace Job
Security
Willing to Give
Defined Expectations
Assistive Management
Merit / Good Pay
Promotion from
wither
Training / Retraining
Jon-Related
Information Job
Security Family
Relationship
Diligence Flexibility /
Move, Retrain
Satisfactory
Performance Lifetime
Employment Loyalty /
Trust
Evolving Social Contract
Employer
Employeer
Expect to Receive
• Ethics & Honesty
• Superior performance
• Continuous Improvement
• Ideas / Participation
• Commitment to business Success
• Personal Investment
• Respect / Participation
• Principled Leadership
• Success based Pay
• Cafeteria Benefits
• Opportunity for Growth
• Learning Climate
• Safe & Healthy Workplace
• Work / life Flexibility
• Secure Transitions
• Trust
Willing to Give
• Trust / Empowerment
• Facilitative Mgmt.
• Variable Pay Earning Opportunity
• Opportunity for Growth
• Cafeteria Benefits
• Learning Support
• Information Access
• Transition Assistance
• Diversity / Work life Programs
• Participation / Involvement
• Willingness to Challenge
• Superior Performance
• Lifelong Learning
• Commitment to Vision
• Business Success

Outline for New Social Contract

Employer Expectations of Employees	Employee Expectations of Employers	Joint Expectations
• Performance to the best of one's ability	• 'Fair' pay and benefits proportionate to contribution to company success	• Partnering replaces paternalism
• Commitment to the objectives of the firm	• Security tied to fortunes of the company and ability to perform	• Employees are value-adding resources
• Participation (suggestions)	• Respect, recognition and participation	• Employee and employer must focus on customer needs and desires
• Willingness to take training to implore productivity	• Opportunities for growth	
• Ethical and honest behaviour	• Access to timely information and openers by candid leaders	
	• Safe and healthy workplace	

Face of New Workplace

The new workplace faces the following key issues and concerns :

1. **Ethics**: A code of moral standards of conduct for what is '**good**' and '**right**' as opposed to what is '**bad**' or '**wrong**'.
2. **Corporate Governance**: The active oversight of management decisions, corporate strategy and financial reportings by the board of Directors.
3. **Globalization**: The worldwide independence of resource flows, product markets and business competition.

   Global Outsourcing: Purchasing products or subcontracting labour to foreign countries.

   Job Migration: The shifting of jobs one country to another.
4. **Diversity:**
   - **Workforce Diversity:** The composition of a workforce in terms of differences among the members, such as gender, age, race, ethnicity, religion, sexual orientation and ableness.
   - **Discrimination**: The holding of negative, irrational attitudes regarding people who are different from us.

- **Prejudice**: The display of negative irrational attitudes toward women and minorities.
- **The glass Ceiling**: An invisible barrier limiting career advancement among women and minorities.

5. **Intellectual Capital**: The collective brain power or shared knowledge of an organization's workforce.

   Intellectual Capital = Competency × Commitment

   - **Knowledge Workers**: Minds and intellects are key assets to employees.
   - **Free Agent Economy** : People change jobs more often and many work as independent contractors for a mix of employees.
   - **Self Management**: The ability to understand oneself, exercise initiative, accept responsibility and learn from experience.
   - **Shamrock Organization**: Operates with a core group of full-time long-term workers supported by others who work on contracts and part-time employees.

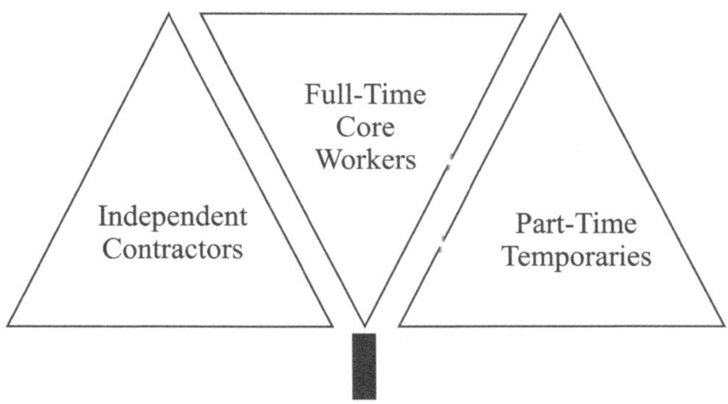

Shamrock Qrganization

New Workplace

The new organization as a workplace consists of:

- **Mission statements** which express the purposes of organizations.
- Organizations are **Open systems** that interact with the environment.
- Qrganizations **Create value** for customers and clients.
- Productivity as a measure of organizational performance.
- Organizations are **changing** as society changes.

Thus, to conclude the following are the Key Transitions in Organisation:

(a) **Less "Command and Control"**: Traditional top-down ways are proving inadequate. The old 'do as I say' bosses are giving way to new 'how I can help you' ones.

(b) **Involvement and Participatory work settings:** The goals are to rally knowledge, experience and commitment of all workers.

(c) **Commitment to Teamwork**: Today's organizations are less vertical and more horizontal in focus. They as more driven by **teamwork** *pooling talents* for creative problem solving.

(d) **Emphasis on Technology**: Changes in computer and information technology bring continuous opportunities. Technology keeps changing the ways organizations operate and people work.

(e) **New workforce expectations**: A new generation of workers is more informal and less tolerant of hierarchy. The new generation tends to value performance merit over status and hierarchy.

20

Ethical Issues in Marketing

The word '**ethics**', known as '**ethikos**' in Greek and '**ethicus**' in Latin, is derived from '**ethos**' which means **character** or **manners**. Ethics is therefore said to be the **science of morals**, **moral principles** and **rules of conduct**.

Marketing is the interface between different and **competing value systems : the firm**, **the customers** and other **people** with whom the business is concerned.

Marketing Management relies on providing products and services that create value for the customers and also satisfy them.

According to Theodre Levitt, "A truly marketing minded firm tries to create value – satisfying goods and services which the consumer will want to buy".

To enable a company to play a responsible role in the society the marketers need to know the role played by ethics in their activities.

Keeping in view the ever-growing importance of consumer orientation in marketing, companies should formulate **code of ethics** that help in framing policies at every level of marketing and where employees can follow uniform standard of ethics.

The characteristics that define acceptable conduct in marketing are called Marketing Ethics.

Factors Influencing Ethical Decision Marking in Marketing

Ferell and Gresham have identified three factors that determine the code of ethics framed by marketer:

1. Individual Factors
2. Significant Factors
3. Opportunity Factors

1. **Individual Factors:** are the moral values inculcated in person by **family, education** and **culture**. The Individual Factors play an important role in framing a marketing decision.
2. **Significant Factors:** refer to the extent to which the **reference groups, top management** and **peers** influence the marketer. These have more to do with the **organizational climate** of the markets.
3. **Opportunity Factors:** are the **ethical codes** and **standards** that are promoted in an organization. They are the **rules** and **policies** framed by organization which all the employees are expected to adhere.

All these factors play an important role in framing a marketing decision.

According to Donaldson and Davis, common ethical standard is important for the **shared values** and to bring **in higher quality** in **products**, **processes** and **services** and for **better output** and **achievement**.

Certain fundamental ethical issues have been codified into statutory regulations, to be followed by manufactures. To nurture their long-term relationship with the customers, they need to conform to ethical standards, which society expects them to follow. If the marketing efforts of a company deviate from these ethical standards it may face serious problems.

Ethical Norms and Values for Marketers

Various Associations and Accrediting bodies have identified guidelines for ethics in marketing.

Norms are established standards of conduct that are expected and maintained by society and professional organizations.

Values represent the collective conception of what people find desirable, important and morally proper. They serve as the criteria for evaluating the actions of other.

The Marketing practitioners must recognize that they not only serve their enterprise but also act as stewards of society in **creating, facilitating** and executing the efficient and effective transactions that all part of the greater economy.

In this role Marketers should embrace the highest ethical norms of practicing professionals and the ethical values implied by their responsibility toward stakeholders (e.g. customers, employees, investors, channel members, regulations and host community).

The American Marketing Association commits itself to promote the highest standard of professional ethical norms and values for its members and have prescribed the following rules to guide marketing behaviour:

1. **Responsibility of the Marketer:** Marketers must accept responsibility for the consequences of their activities and make every effort to ensure that their decisions recommendations, and actions function to identify, serve, and satisfy all relevant publics: customers, organizations and society.
2. Honest, Integrity and Quality are important than quick profits.
3. **Rights and Duties in Marketing Exchange Process**: The participants should be able to expect that products and services are safe and fit for intended uses; that communications about offered products and services are not deceptive; that all parties intend to discharge their obligations financial or otherwise in **good faith**; and appropriate internal methods exist for equitable adjustment or redress of grievances concerning purchases.
4. **Organizational Relationships:** Marketers should be aware of how their behaviour influences the behaviour of others in organizational relationships. They should not demand, encourage or apply coercion to encourage unethical behaviour in their relationships with others.
5. Conduct your business so as to build long-terms loyalty. It is essential to build a sales relationship which lasts for years and create a stream referral business.
6. **Marketers must do no harm.** This means doing work for which they are appropriately trained or experienced to add value to their organizations and customers. It also means adhering to all applicable laws and regulations and embodying high ethical standards in the choice they make.

7. Marketers must foster **trust** in the marketing system. The marketing communications about goads and services should not be deceptive or misleading. It implies for good faith and fair dealing so as to contribute toward the efficacy of the exchange process.
8. **Marketers** must **embrace, communicate** and **practice** the fundamental ethical values that will improve **consumer confidence** in the integrity of the marketing exchange system. These basic values includes **honesty, responsibility, fairness, respect, openers and citizenship.**

ETHICAL ISSUES IN MARKETING-MIX IN ENVIRONMENT FRAMEWORK

The elements of Marketing Mix i.e. **Product, Price, Place** and **Promotion** evolves and relates to the environmental factors i.e.:

1. Competitive Environment
2. Political-legal Environment
3. Socio-cultural Environment
4. Economic Environment
5. Technological Environment

Within these environmental factors the various marketing mix elements and their ethical perspective is to be analysed:

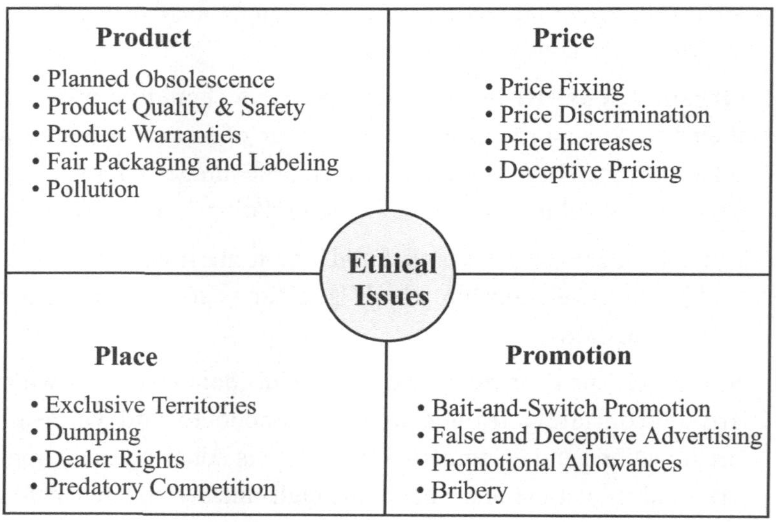

1. Ethical Issues Relating to Product

Product is the first element in the marketing mix. Various decisions are involved in the Product element such as:

1. Quality of Product
2. Safety of Product
3. Packaging and Branding Issues
4. Product Warranties

These issues are of vital importance and does have certain ethical obligations associated to it:

1. **Quality of Product**: The demand for high-quality products is of key issue. It is a general responsibility of the business to ensure that the quality of a product measures up to the claims made about it and to reasonable consumer expectation.
2. **Safety of Product**: The business should give safety the priority warranted by the product. However, the businesses often base safety considerations strictly on cost. If the margin of safety can be increased without significantly disturbing budgetary considerations, then it is fine but if not then the safety questions appears.

Two factors of safety are associated with cost which cannot be ignored:

(a) The **seriousness of the injury** the product can cause.

(b) The **frequency of its concrescence**.

When a product scores high on both the seriousness and frequency tests, it warrants the highest priority as a potential safety hazard.

The safety of a product can also be ensured by **monitoring the manufacturing process** itself by the business. The companies should also periodically review the working conditions and competence of key personal.

The safety engineers should ensure product safety.

3. **Packaging and Branding Issues**: Ethical issues in product also involves two other major attributes of product i.e. the **Packaging** and **Branding Attribute**.

   It is an ethical responsibility of the manufacturer to provide clear, accurate and adequate information regarding the labeling and packaging of products. Nothing is more misleading than environmental labeling. Manufacturers label products as "biodegradable", "environmentally safe" or "recyclable" without defining the terms.

The consumers have long been equally baffled by food labels such as "light" or "97% fact free", "Cholesterol-Free" etc.

The ethics suggests that the manufactures should provide exact and correct information regarding the ingredients used in the product.

The packaging should be such that the manufacturer's real is ensured and that the product quantity should also be exactly measured and provided.

There should not be any misleading information regarding the quantity and quality of the product.

4. **Product Warranties** : one way that business assumes responsibilities to consumers for product quality and reliability is through **warranties,** which are obligations to purchasers that sellers assume. The ethics relates to two kinds of warranties.

   (a) **Express Warranties :** are the claims that sellers explicitly state-for example, that a product is "shrinkproof" or will require no maintains for some years. The moral/ethical concern of the business is whether a product lives up to its statements. Express warranties include assertions about the product's character, assurances of product durability, and other statements on warranty cards, labels, wrappers and packages or in the advertising of the product.

   (b) **Implied Warranties:** include the claim, implicit in any sale, that a product is fit for its ordinary, intended use. The law calls this the implied warranty of **merchantability**. It's not a promise that the product will be perfect rather it's a guarantee that it will be of passable quality or suitable of the ordinary purpose for which it is used. **Implied Warranties** are more specific.

   Thus, the ethics demands that the manufacturers must fulfill the product warranty needs.

2. Ethical Issues Relating to Price

Business, as well as governments and non-government organization (NGO$^{s'}$), employ a wide range of pricing tactics. Many are genuine inducements to entice potential purchasers, or to encourage a particular behaviour. But others seek to mislead deliberately or simply to make the deal seem better than it really is. But even legal practices can produce changes in buyer or distributor behaviour that lead to undesired consequences.

The following are the unethical pricing practices:

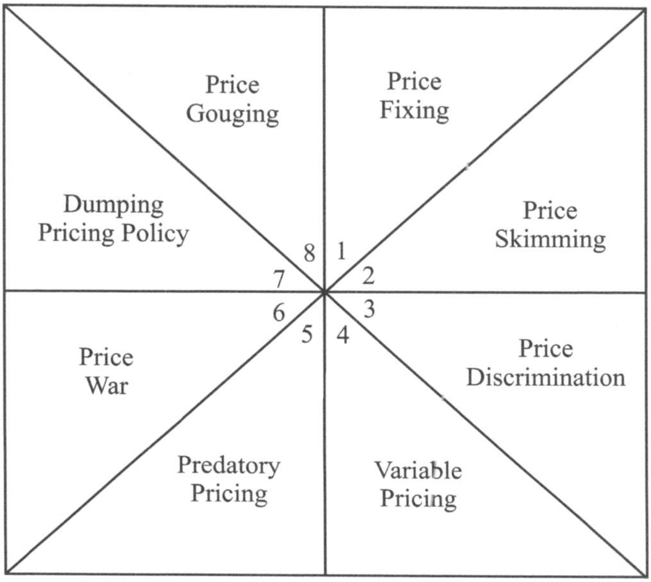

Unethical Pricing Practices

1. **Price Fixing**: is an agreement between business competitors to sell the same product or service at the same price. It is an agreement intended to push the price of a product as high as possible, leading to profits for all the sellers. **Price Fixing** is illegal, however some governments even sanction it, particularly in countries which have developing economies.

2. **Price Skimming:** is a pricing strategy in which a marketer **sets a relatively high price** for a product or service at first, then lowers the price over time.

3. **Price Discrimination:** exists when sales of identical goods or services are transacted at different prices from the same provider. It also occurs when it costs more to supply one customer than it does another, and yet the supplies charges both the same price.

4. **Variable Pricing:** The alternative of fixed price policy is **Variable Pricing**, which is a form of **first degree price discrimination,** characterized by **individual bargaining** and **negotiation**.

   Two variants of Variable Pricing are (a) **Price Shading** (in which sales people are given the authority to vary the price by a certain amount or percentage). (b) **Auctions** is which potential buyers have the option of bidding on a product and thereby varying the price.

5. **Predatory Pricing:** also known as destroyer pricing is the practice of a firm selling a product at very low price with the intent of driving competitors out of the market or create a barrier to entry into the market for potential new competitors.
6. **Price War**: is used to indicate a state of intense competitive rivalry accompanied by a multi-lateral **series of price reductions**. One competitor will lower its price, then others will lower their prices to match.
7. **Dumping Pricing Policy** : It is used in the context of international trade, where dumping is defined as the act of a manufacturer in one country exporting a product to another country at a price which is either below the price it charges in its home market or below its costs of production.
8. **Price Gouging** : is a reference to a seller's asking a price that is much higher than what is seen as '**fair**' under the circumstances.

ETHICAL ISSUES RELATING TO PLACE

By '**place**' marketers refer to the sum of locations by which the product moves from the supplier to the consumer.

'**Place**' is a point at which the customers is able to access the information about a particular product or service and get the final product.

'**Place**' also includes the process of distributing the product and the type of delivery service that is offered to the final consumer.

Unethical practices arise in "**Place**" when the marketer adopts:

1. **Distribution to Exclusive Territories:** i.e. when the marketer distributes products to certain restricted or exclusive territories.

   Unethical practices may also arise when the marketer stops distribution at a particular place because of not yielding profits. Consumers who frequently purchase a particular product from that particular place are deprived of getting the product from the desired place. Customers who regularly buy products from those places will have to depend on other places to get the products of their choice.
2. **Dealer Rights :** Another ethical issue relates to the rights given to the dealers. The marketers may at times give exclusive rights of distributions to only certain dealers, which may misuse such right.

3. **Dumping:** Due to open market another unethical issue relates to the **dumping policy** of certain countries. It is the act of a manufacturer in one country exporting a product to another country at a price which is lower than the country wherein they want to dump the products. In such a case the products may be available at a cheap rates.

Ethical Issues Relating to Promotion

All companies use **advertising** and **public relations** strategies to attract more customers. The method that a company adopts to promote its products and the way it communicates to its customers are subjected to lose scrutiny by consumers and by the advertising code of ethics.

Advertising is considered unethical when:

1. It **degrades** the **rival's product** or **substitute product**
2. It gives **misguiding information**
3. It gives **false information**
4. It **conceals information** that vitally affects the human life (e.g. side effects of drugs, precautions which using a geyser etc.)
5. It is **obscene** or **immoral**

Ethical advertising contains truth, not absolute truth but socially accepted standards of honesty as truth. It has to be right in its approach and claims.

Ethical advertising can shift the demand curve to the right; unethical can shift the demand curve of the firm to the left.

Unethical Advertising can take the following forms:

1. **Untruthful Claims:** Ads offering mixtures and substances which promises **loss of weight, growth of hair**, **growth in height**, **sexual energy**, **freedom** and **independence** make patently false claims.
2. **Exaggerated Claims:** The exaggeration in consumer advertising is not only in the headlines, body copy and slogans but also in the strong visuals. The mouth-watering visuals of T.V. Ads of ice-creams, cakes, biscuits, chocolates, jellies, yogart etc. are created with 'models' that have nothing to do with the look, the feel and the taste of the product.
3. **Unverifiable Claims** in a language that is Ambiguous : Advertisements of '**energy drinks**' (Horlicks, Maltora etc.) tells us about the number of vitamins and how they help children to grow strong and tall. There is just no way of verifying these tall claims.

4. **The use of misleading labels and names:** The Indian advertisers have to the frequently warned by the Multinational Companies not to use the brand names and labels of their products.
5. **The use of Testimonials or Endorsements:** The advertises pay huge amount of fees to film and sports personalities who have nothing to do with the use of the product or the service, to endorse their products.
6. **Creating Erroneous Impressions:** Advertisers frequently exploit the heapness of Indians for 'foreign' products by giving foreign brands names such is '**Park Aveme**' or '**Combridge**' to their products or by getting Europeans or Americans to endorse Indian products.

   Some manufactures advertise indigenous cosmetics and perfumes by using names like '**France**' or '**Paris**' or '**Cologne**' in their advertisements to create the erroneous impression that such products are '**foreign**'.
7. **The use of women** to advertise products that are targeted at men-products as cars, bikes, after shave lotions, etc. The women are seductively used to advertise the products.
8. **Alcohol and Tobacco Advertising:** Advertising of alcoholic drinks and tobacco are prohibited in the broadcasting media. The advertisers violate all these prohibitions in ingenious ways.

   Such advertising has made its appearance indirectly through advertising of soda, glasses and mineral water. These indirect ads are called as **Surrogate advertising**.

   Firms like McDonell sponsor sport events and promote their brands of liquor. Sponsorship of sports events and historical places have been commonly used by the manufacturers.

   These are various unethical advertising strategies used by the manufacturers to attract consumers.

CONCLUSION

Thus **Marketing Ethics** is the moral evaluation of marketing activities and decisions as right or wrong. Marketing behaviour is judged as ethical or unethical on the basis of commonly accepted principles of behaviour established by the expectations of society, various interest groups, competitors, organization's management and individual's personal moral values.

An ethical violations make continued trust in marketing exchanges difficult.

21

Whistle-Blowing

As there are certain obligations of companies to their employees, in the same way there are some obligations of employees to their employers.

When an employee publicly exposes an employer's misconduct, that act is called "**WHISTLE-BLOWING**".

The metaphor is drawn from the world of sports and refers to when a referee announces a foul by blowing a whistle, stopping play and assessing a penalty.

Similarly, on employee who **reports frond**, **waste** or an employee's illegal activities not only brings the reported behaviour to a stop but also causes the company to be penalized by regulatory agencies or the courts or be subject to other government action, when to engage in such behaviour and the consequences that follow from it are essential to consider in business ethics.

Some writers in business ethics see whistle-blowing as any **act of reporting corporate wrong-doing**, regardless of the position of the one doing the reporting.

Thus, it includes acts of public reporting by **journalists, public interest groups** even a **single individual** who becomes aware of activity that is either harmful, illegal or both.

For example, suppose a particular firm exposes toxic gases to the environment, which was not known by any other person excluding the employees of the company, in that situation it the employee pronounce it in the public, is regarded as an act of **whistle-blowing**.

Complicating the individual's decision whether or not to become a whistle-blower is the fact that- *not all allegations made by whistle – blowers are correct.*

To engage in whistle-blowing is to be labeled as a trouble-maker, for sometimes whistle-blowers make unsubstantiated accusations in an effort to retaliate gains an employer for real or imagined grievances.

What better way to cause a business organization an immense amount of discomfort then to make allegation of wrong-doing, especially when the whistle-blower claim moral superiority and is often protected by state and law. The laws designed to protect whistle-blowing can be criticized as encouraging frivolous retaliatory actions by unhappy employees.

Some critics have also charged that protective legislation undermines the loyalty that a business organization must expect if it is to function.

Facets of Whistle-Blowing

Whistle-blowing, being the conduct of reporting work for the betterment of the entire society as a whole, has the following **characteristics:**

1. The reporter should be an integral part i.e. the employee of the business organization but this condition is not mandatory, even the journalist or any other social interest group or an individual can undertake this activity. For example, Medha Patkar in the Environment Protection. Menaka Gandhi in Wildlife Protection, etc.
2. The **whistle-blowing activity** should be undertaken within the parameters of the company loyalty.
3. The **reporting work should** be **channelised** in a **proper way-unbiased exposition**. The reporting mechanism should be conducted in such a way that it can attract the major segments of the society or well recognized by organized society.
4. The **timing of whistle-blowing**: the exposition of bad behaviour or bad conduct in a specific point of time should be done which will mutually

benefit the largest segment of the society. The proper timings of declarations can marginalise the role of the company in the negative directions and saves the most valuable ethical works or obligations of the company.

Thus, the whistle-blowing is the voluntary expositions of non-public informations as a moral protest by a member or former member of an organization, outside the normal member of an organizaton, outside the normal channel of communication to an appropriate (media) audience, about the illegal or immoral conduct that is opposed in some significant way to the public interest.

In the context of whistle-blowing three terms are to be understood with:- Loyalty, Fidelity and Honesty.

American Philosopher Kurt Baier defined fidelity as an agent's willingness to promote the interests ahead of the interests of others due to the agent's obligations to that someone.

In other words, an employee incurs an obligation to the employer by accepting employment. The relation b/w employer and employee can be considered as the contractual one i.e. in return of the agent's (employee's) labour, creativity and time – the employer gives payments (wages, benefits). The employee has incurred and obligation in return to many that includes giving full effort to the job and being honest in all the dealing with the firm (not to lie, steal or cheat). Failure to carry through on this incurred obligation would be an example of lack of fidelity.

An additional obligation of an employee is to put the interests of the employer's business above that of other agencies or firms or business. Failure to do so would be an example of failing in loyalty.

The loyalty and fidelity can be treated as a binary fashion given-and-take relationship.

Fidelity is the obligations towards the work, while **loyalty** is the obligation towards the entire organization or the employer as a whole. The employer should not do anything which will marginalise or diminish the dignity of the company as a whole.

The lack of loyalty creates JOB-SWITCHING which is most prevalent practice in Indian, American and British Companies. But such a practice is an exception in Japanese, where the culture is to stick to the work position for the lifetime, which can be further extended to next generations.

Moral decisions would be easies of we were bound by the ties of loyalty to only one person or an organization. But it is not so easy, we have to incur obligations of loyalty to employer but also have obligations to others like family members. Friends, co-workers, to the government and to the society as a whole.

It is not always easy to know where our obligation for one person or group ends and where our obligation to another person or oranization begins.

The difficulty of dealing with this issue to make the decision i.e., of to blow the whistle or not — so difficult. It raises the issue of choosing among competing loyalties.

Duties to an Employer

By freely accepting employment one incurs both **responsibilities** and **duties**. An individual (employee) obligates itself to work for the employer, to deliver his best, both in terms of time and talent and to put the interest of the employer above that of other business firms.

According to two Contemporary Writers **Norma Bowie** and **Ronald Duska**, "Each job carries with it a responsibility or obligation to do what the job or role demands. This is because either there is – an explicit contract with a very detailed / complete description of the job and its obligations; or there is a less formal agreement where the employee agrees to do what is in the best interest of the principal or of the employer."

The following are the key duties to be undertaken by an employee which is also anticipated by the employer:

1. My Station and Its Duties

F. H. Bradley argues that each of us has a 'station' in life that brings with it certain set of duties and obligations (for e.g.) to be a student in a class means that he has a set of obligations which may be different from one who is a parent/teacher.

Bradeley's analysis emphasises that each of us may have a different set of duties depending on our station. This nation also points to another important moral principle- one is morally responsible only for that which one can do. (To save a person from drowning you need to know to swim but you can help him by calling for help from lifeguards etc.).

One can be morally held responsible for events that are within your power.

2. Do no Harm

It leads to the principle that we have moral obligations to avoid harm. If a company makes a product with defects, society reacts with a sense of moral outrage at the company's failure to prevent death that were foreseeable and avoidable.

The 2 basic principles are **loyalty to on employer** and the **duty to avoid harm**.

So there arises the difficulty of knowing precisely which of these two conflicting moral principles takes precedence in our decision-making.

Further, complicating a decision about whistle-blowing is the "role of self-interest."

3. Self-Interest and Whistle-Blowing

Kurt Baier says more strongly when he observes that a moral point of view is precisely required to override the self-interest.

He emphasises that the universal obedience to certain rules, over-riding self-interests would produce a state of affairs which serves everyone's interests. (so it means that concept of self-interest should be avoided.)

It is the self-interest which dilutes the moral principles in the decision-making.

Thus, the moral principle in whistle-blowing is the **abandonment** of the principle of self-interest.

If any kind of self-interest is considered as a part o whistle-blowing practice, then it is not considered as a moral principle/act.

The reporter (whistle-blower) should be free from any kind of personal biasness, in connection with the exposition of the moral conduct actively involved in the materialistic world.

Thus, in a nutshell-it is not easy to be a WHISTLE-BLOWER. According to a Research study in the U.S.A., more than 54% of the whistle-blowers are generally harassed by their press and while 25% of the whistle-blowers argued that the family pressure is the most powerful ingredient which compels the employee to abstain from whistle-blowing. Thus, this activity has lost its identity in the race of truth.

Protection for Whistle-Blowers

The bold and courageous steps taken by the whistle-blowers should be protected from each and every only, so that the social pattern or the social system can be rationally protected. Each and every person working in the system sometimes dares to expose the loopholes, faults or misdeeds of their firm. As a result of which nobody dares to undertake unethical practices. The following are certain *protective measures* to be undertaken to *protect the whistle-blower*.

1. The name of the whistle-blower should be kept in secret.
2. Sufficient legal protections or anarchments should be ensured.
3. The family members as well as the property of the whistle-blowers should be taken under the judicial authority custody and it should be ensured that no illegal actions can be initiated against the whistle-blowers and his family.
4. If the employer undertakes any kind of malicious activities to suppress the whistle-blower, then it is the obligation of the government or the regulatory authorities to make sure that no financial as well as mental torture should be done to the whistle-blower. As a nutshell, it can be recommended that star network can be encircled to the whistle-blower and some encouraging rewards should be granted so that the culture or activity of whistle-blowing spreads over rather than deliberately marginalising the whistle-blowing activities (whistle-blowing culture should be developed).
5. The social response as well as obligations should be channelised to encourage and protect the truth-tellers and his position should be at the premium level in the society (he should become an idol for the society). For example, the FERA Act. The Company's Act, The SEBI Act, etc. enacted to protect the whistle-blowers (the Indian Penal Code).

The Questions of the Whistle-Blowers

Three important questions are related with the whistle-blowers, which could be analysed:-

1. What can I do?

This question relates to Self-Appraisal (First, appraise yourself that whether I am capable to do the particular work, Am I authorized to be the work or to blow-whistle). Try to put yourself in the position of the opponent also.

2. Am I forced to blow the whistle?

This question implies that whether you are getting impending threats by internal consciousness. It should be your own idea. There should be on fear of punishment. You should feel that it is your responsibility to blow the whistle.

3. Are the Issues Momentus

Whether it really deserves to blow the whistle or not. What is the relative importance of a particular issues in a particular time or situation. Whether the issue needs to be exposed or whether an act is worth for alarming the firm, society at large or not.

The Cost Whistle-Blowing

The whistle-blowing concept though is nobel, no individual employee dares to pick up there kinds of activities by keeping in mind various intended threats, which may be imposed upon.

Since, the employee is a part of the organization and bounds to work under the guidance or control of the employer, nobody generally likes to expose the misdeeds or the drawbacks or flows of the employer.

However, there are certain moderately religious or principled persons who initiates in the whistle-blowing activity without taking into consideration any kinds of threats.

But, still there is an ethical principle in this connection which suggests that the **Cost-Benefit Analysis** of the whistle-blowing should be analysed and if the benefits supersedes the cost then the whistle-blowing is recommended otherwise the employee should abstain himself from there activities.

However, if an employee followed only the principle of self-interest then one would never become a whistle-blower for the costs can include loss of employment, loss of esteem of co-workers and even decline in one's emotional and physical health. Laws such as FALSE CLAIMS ACT, however are intended to provide a powerful incentive to the whistle blower who is proved to be false.

The following are the various costs associated with the whistle-blows:-

1. **Retrenchment** or **work position** is in **danger**.

2. The **colleagues** or the **contemporary workers** may not extend the cooperation with the whistle-blower.
3. Third cost, is associated with **some financial punishments** which may be imposed either in the way of cash or kind for e.g., **Penalties.**
4. The whistle-blower may be confronted with a **non-nurturing system** or **non-cooperative system**, i.e., he my be regarded/treated as an untouchable.
5. **Family praise** of **Family burden** can be another **cost**. Most of the employees are generally overburdened with family pressure / issues. As an employee have extensive liabilities towards their family members so he has to reconsider his act to blow the whistle or not. As a social being an employee who is not under the family pressures can act as a good whistle-blower.

Thus, a company's business ethics are its self-established standards for its relationships with the employees, customers and the community as a whole.

It is the fabric describing the integrity as values of a business as exhibited by its leadership and its employees.

Moreover, good business ethics leads to improved products and services improved employee performance and greater customer loyalty.

The continued well-being of a business depends upon strong respect and supports for its products and services by its employees and **customer's loyalty is the glue which binds these separate** constituents to a business. Good ethics is the source and catalyst for this loyalty.

22

Ethical Responsibilities of Business Towards Consumers and Employees

Business plays a very significant role in economic, social, political and technological affairs. So the business owes responsibilities to all segments of society.

The businesses can succeed only if they maintain good relationships with all their stakeholders. The relationship can be strengthened if organizations fulfill their obligations towards their stakeholders.

The various stakeholders includes:- Shareholders, employees, management, consumers, suppliers, creditors, competitors and community.

Responsibility is an **obligations of decision–maker** to take actions which protect and improve the welfare of society as a whole along with their own interests.

Social responsibility of business means the obligation of business enterprises to make decision and follow lines of action which are desirable in terms of the objectives and values of society.

Ethical Responsibilities of Business Towards Consumers

The marketplace where consumer products are sold is a very complex institution.

The responsibilities of business corporations towards their consumers are to provide the products at:-

1. The Right Quality
2. The Right Quantity
3. At Right Time
4. At Right Place
5. At Right Price

The responsibilities can also be summed up as:-

1. Producing goods according to the specific needs of consumers, their purchasing power etc.
2. Offering quality goods at reasonable prices.
3. Improving the standard of living by producing goods and services of high quality.
4. Treating customers fairly in all aspects of business transactions.
5. Ensuring the health and safety of customers.
6. After sales services are available.
7. To inform and educate consumers on the arrival and use of products.
8. To be honest and truthful in the matter of advertising and warranty.
9. To offer improved and new products through technical and marketing research.
10. To avoid monopolistic and restrictive trade practices.
11. Ensuring that the product promotion and advertising are not misleading.
12. **Trust** forms the basis of successful marketplace transactions and is the most important ethical issue.

It is the responsibility of the business to make sure that this trust of consumers is not shaken, that the products they serve are safe to use and will give consumers the value they expect.

Consumer is the foundation of business and satisfaction of Consumers is the raison d'eter of business activities. This implies much more than the supply of goods and services.

Various unfair practices like hoarding, adulteration, shoddy merchandise, unfair measurements, misleading advertising etc. reveals, that many business firm fail to fulfill their obligations to consumers.

ETHICAL RESPONSIBILITIES OF BUSINESS TOWARDS EMPLOYEES

A legal contract of employment governs the relationship between the organization and the employee. This relationship is considered to be important to society, because employees contribute their efforts and time towards the development of the organization, which improves the society.

The employment contract places certain responsibility towards their employees. In return for their work employee expect **wages, benefits** and **security**. And it is the responsibility of the organization to meet their expectation.

Most Japanese corporations provide security to their employees by offering lifetime employment.

Many organizations also try to ensure the growth and well-being of their employees during the period of the employment.

Some firms regularly conduct training programmes not only to enhance employee's skills but also to help them move in the hierarchy.

Some specific responsibilities of organizations towards their employees are:-

1. To provide adequate compensation, fair wages or salary for the contribution made.
2. To provide for good working condition i.e., safe and clean drinking water facilities, proper lightning, ventilation etc. that respect each employee's health and dignity.
3. To be honest in communication with employees and open in sharing information.
4. To redress employee grievances regularly. To listen to and where possible, act on employee suggestions, ideas, requests and complaint.
5. To engage in negotiations when conflict arises.
6. To avoid discriminatory practices and guarantee equal treatment and opportunity regardless of gender, age, race and religion.
7. To encourage and assist employees in developing skills and knowledge that are required for accomplishing the task.
8. To provide opportunity for advancement and self-improvement.
9. To ensure that employees have job satisfaction by making work worthwhile and not routine or challenging.
10. To involve and participate the employees in the managerial decision making process.

23

Employee Discrimination

EMPLOYEE DISCRIMINATION

Words such as 'justice', 'equality', 'racism', 'rights' and 'discrimination' are becoming the buzzwords.

Some of the unethical practices in hiring of an employee are related to the discrimination. So the first step towards ethical selection is to prevent discrimination. Adequate care should be taken to see that this discrimination is based on relevant criteria.

The root meaning of the term 'discriminate' is 'to distinguish one object from another', a morally neutral and not necessarily wrongful activity. However, in modern usage the term is not morally neutral. It refers to the wrongful act of distinguishing illicitly among people not on the basis of individual merit but on the basis of prejudice or some other invidious or morally reprehensible attitude.

To discriminate in employment is to make an adieus decision (or set of decisions) against employees (or prospective employees) who belong to a certain class because of morally unjustified prejudice towards members of that class.

Discrimination in employment thus, must involve **3 basic elements**:-

1. It is a decision against one or more employees (or prospective employees) that is not based on individual merit such as the ability to perform a given job, seniority or other morally legitimate qualifications.
2. Secondly, the decision derives solely or in part from racial or sexual prejudice, from false stereotypes, or from some other kind of morally unjustified attitude against members of the class to which the employee belongs.
3. Third, the decision (or set of decisions) has a harmful or negative impact on the interests of the employees, costing them jobs, promotions, or better pay.

Thus, judging a person's functional abilities or qualities on the basis of age, gender, religion, nationality or social background is considered discriminatory.

Discrimination means unequal treatment. It implies violation of right to equality. It means giving privileges to a few and dinging just and fair treatment to all. It has several forms like social, legal, economic or discrimination at work-place etc. The concept of discrimination in its strict sense implies an unjust or unequal treatment to a single person or a class of persons.

FEATURES OF DISCRIMINATION

Some of the important features of discrimination are as follows:-

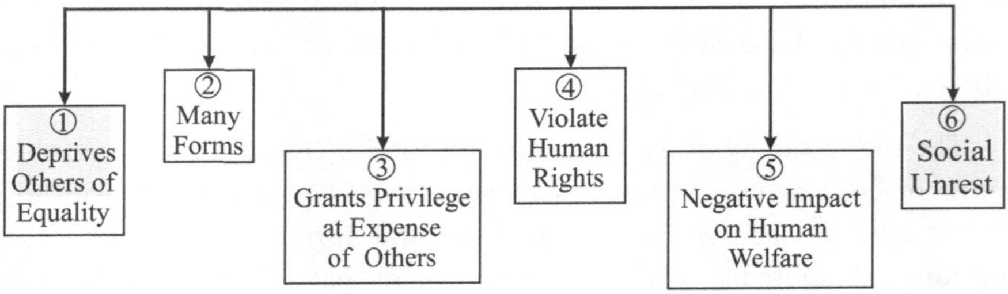

1. **Deprives Others of Equality:** The outstanding feature of discrimination is not to give all an equal treatment or consideration. It is an act of violating principles of equality as well as justice.
2. **May Forms:** Discrimination has many forms. A person or group may be discriminated on several basis like **age, race, gender, religion, colour, nationality, origin** or **beauty** etc. Therefore, discrimination may prevail in different forms like **social, legal, economic** or **individual discrimination.**

3. **Grants privilege at Expense of Others:** The basic cause of discrimination is to dory someone his due rights and treatment so as to give a preferential treatment to others. The core of discrimination is robbing one of his rights to provide concessions to others.
4. **Violate Human Rights:** Discrimination always involves depending a person or class from their rights. It also includes violation of human rights like right of equality, justice, freedom of expression and thought and other civil liberties. Discrimination also hurts the natural freedom and dignity of a person.
5. **Negative Impact on Human Welfare:** Discrimination is opposite of equality. It involves unequal treatment of a person or class of persons on basis of some erroneous assumptions about a person or class. It reduces self-confidence amongst the discriminated.
6. **Social Unrest:** The most dangerous impact of discrimination is the social unrest. It harts the inner feelings and the discriminated classes breed a sense of revenge against other classes. They even turn hostile and do not leave a chance to cause damage to others. Discrimination causes riots, massacres and social disturbances.

TYPE OF DISCRIMINATION

The various types of discrimination are:-

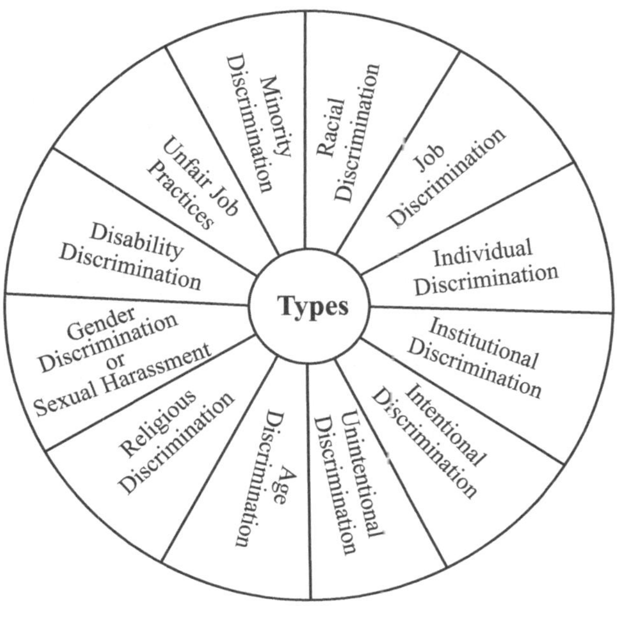

1. **Individual Discrimination:** Discrimination may be by person to another. It also includes discrimination by an institution. Individual discrimination means unequal treatment by a person to another person or a class of persons.
2. **Institutional Discrimination:** Institutional discrimination means unequal treatment by an organization to an individual or group. **For example** : If a company has a policy not to recruit Asians, it is an institutional discrimination, whereas of the Personal Manager has a personal bias against the Asians, it is Individual Discrimination.
3. **Intentional Discrimination:** Discrimination may be a deliberate attempt to treat unequally. It may also happen without any intention to do so. For example, the Recruiting Officer may not like to recruit females, so during the interview he may put difficult questions to them. Such treatment is intentional discrimination.
4. **Unintentional Discrimination:** Where a person unknowingly treats another differently it is unintentional discrimination.
5. **Minority Discrimination:** Where a person belonging to a minority group of population is not equally treated as compared to the persons belonging to majority of population, it is called MINORITY DISCRIMINATION. The basis of minority discrimination may be region, religion, caste, creed, nationality or race or gender etc. In several societies people are treated unequally because they belong to a religious or social minority groups or caste based groups.
6. **Age Discrimination:** The attempt of employees to employ people of a specific age group like 'young' or 'college students' without any specific requirement of the job is called **age discrimination**. It also includes instances to remove employees by involuntary retirement who have not attained the upper protected limit of age. It also includes discrimination to award pension and other terminal benefit plans to employees on the basis of age. An employer has to award terminal benefits equally to employees regardless of their age.
7. **Religious Discrimination:** It means treating employees differently on the basis of their religious faith or moral or ethical beliefs. It includes disregarding the religious sentiments like religious holidays, prayer break during work, special dress etc. of people belonging to other religious.
8. **Gender Discrimination or Sexual Harassment:** Unequal treatment or granting privileges on the basis of sex or gender implies **gender discrimination.** It includes sexual harassment either **by conditioning**

job benefits or by **creating hostile work environment**. If an employer tries to sexually exploit its employees either by '**quit pro quo**' i.e. unwelcome sexual advances or requests for sexual farness; or by '**hostile environment**' i.e. creating offensive working condition, then it is called as **Sexual Harassment/Discrimination.** Examples like separate promotion or seniority criteria for women, different wage or pension or fringe benefits, barring woman on certain jobs as per marital status or those having minor children or differently treating pregnant women come under sexual discrimination.

9. **Disability Discrimination:** Disability means those suffering from physical or mental impairment of a person within the limit prescribed by law. For example, polio affected leys, deafness, poor vision or suffering from diseases that partially affects work and efficiency of a person fall under physical disability. Different laws in different countries protect rights of physical disabled person by ensuring an equal treatment. For example, in India job are reserved for blind and disabled persons.
10. **Unfair Job Practices:** Job Discrimination may be resorted by retaliatory or unlawful or unfair job practices. Examples of such discrimination are prohibition to oppose unlawful action or discrimination, reporting complaints against illegal discrimination and seeking legal remedy against unlawful job practices.
11. **Racial Discrimination:** Unequal treatment or maltreatment on the basis of race is called **racial discrimination**. Due to Apartheid, in America and South Africa blacks were treated as slaves and inferior to whites. They were subjected to social isolation and were discriminated in schools, in jobs, at places of worship etc.
12. **Job Discrimination:** It means unequal treatment to employees at place of work. The reason for unequal treatment could be age, religion, colour, nationality or other factors not relevant to job requirement.

Measures to Eliminated Discrimination

The important measures to eliminate discrimination can be categorized as:-

1. Legal Measures
2. Affirmative Action

1. **Legal Measures:** Various laws and Acts have been devised to

eliminate discrimination from workplace by the government. These can be summarised as:-

1. Factories Act, 1948	It provides for health, safety and welfare measure of workers.
2. Minimum Wages Act, 1948	It protects minimum wages for workers.
3. Payment of Wages Act, 1936	It governs provision for payment of wages.
4. Payment of Bonus Act, 1965	It requires payment of bonus to employees.
5. Workmen's Compensation Act, 1923	It provides for compensation, if a worker sustains an injury while on job.
6. Employee State Insurance Act, 1938	It requires owners to contribute for insurance of employees.
7. Equal Remuneration Act, 1976	It requires payment of equal wages for equal work.
8. Bounded Labour System (Abolition) Act, 1976	It bans bounded labour system.
9. Civil Right Act, 1991	It provides for punitive liability for discrimination on basis of gender or disability.
10. Equal Pay Act, 1963	It requires payment of equal pay for equal work.

2. **Affirmative Action:** Affirmative action comprises such measures that help to eliminate discrimination of women and minority groups. Some of the affirmative actions are:-

1. **Active Recruitment :** Active recruitment of members of minorities and women is one of the affirmative actions to eliminate discrimination.
2. **Training:** Adequate training be imparted to women and minority members so as to be able to compete the other class of people. It is also necessary to make them aware of their rights and means of redressal.
3. **Promotion:** In order to weed out social bias of discrimination promotions to women and minority member may be given so that they search to higher post. For this purpose some reservation of quota system may be introduced.
4. **Job Safety:** An important concern relating to employees or workers is safety while on job. In industrial units workers are exposed to risky or hazardous operations or process and therefore need to be protected. Organizations must not discriminate employees on account of job safety measures.
5. **Health and Occupations Safety:** Employees should not be indifferent to provide for health safety by way of installing health safe guard gadgets and protective instruments as headgear, spectacle etc. and various other measures should also be adopted to avoid occupational diseases.

Thus, affirmative action implies a set of specific, result-oriented procedures designed to achieve equal employment opportunity. The objective of an affirmative action program is to achieve within a reasonable period of time an employee work fore that in all occupational categories reflects the makeup of the relevant labour market. Affirmative action programs establish specific goals and timetables designed to accomplish this objective.

Job Discrimination or Discrimination of Employees

Job discrimination involves all such instances where an employee or a class is given a preferential treatment on some unjust reasons. According to Fredrick and Lawrence discrimination in jobs is, "unequal treatment of employees based on non job related factors as race, sex, age, national origin, religion, colour and physical or mental handicap." Thus, job discrimination is unequal treatment on a basis not related to the job or work.

Types of Job Discrimination

All types of job discrimination may be divided in two categories:-

Common Causes	Causes Inside Organisation
	• Out of Turn Promotion • Special Benefits • Unfair Allocation of Work • Unfair Working Hours • Unfair Placement and Transfer • Obstructing Change of Work • Personal Bias of Superior • Nepotism • Reservation Policy • Internal Reasons

I. Common Causes

The common types of job discrimination are **individual, institutional, intentional, unintentional, minority, social** or **gender** based discrimination.

II. Causes Inside Organization

Other types of job discrimination may be attributed to unequal treatment in giving opportunities and privileges, which are as follows:-

- **(i) Out of Turn Promotion:** Implies placing a person at a higher position or level ignoring the other senior and equally competent employees.
- **(ii) Special Benefits:** If a person in employment is given special or extra benefit or advantages in comparison to others, it is a form of **job discrimination**.
- **(iii) Unfair Allocation of Work:** If there is no equitable distribution of work amongst employees i.e. some are burdened with work while others are given little work, it is **job discrimination.**
- **(iv) Unfair Working Hours:** If all employees are not given similar working hours i.e. some are given 8 hours of work while other are given the concession to work for shorter hours for similar wages, it is a discrimination on basis of working hours.
- **(v) Unfair Placement and Transfer:** All employees of some category must be placed on difficult and easier jobs on rotation. If one or few employees are regularly placed on difficult and risky jobs while other are assigned simple and easy jobs, it is discrimination.

(vi) **Obstructing Change of Work:** Sometimes an organization binds some employees and does not allow to change their employment which may be considered as job discrimination also, For example, certain company's policies suggest a contract of employment for firs five years or so.

(vii) **Personal Bias of Superior:** If a superior treats one or some of his subordinates in preference to others, it is known as **Preferential Job Discrimination**. Such discrimination may be based upon personal thinking of the superior.

(viii) **Reservation Policy:** If an organization keeps some benefits or privileges as to recruitment, promotion, transfer etc. to a class of employees it amounts to job discrimination. However, reservation of scheduled castes, tribes and backward classes is as per the provisions of our constitution and is not a job discrimination.

Measurement of Job Discrimination

The magnitude and impact of job discrimination may be more or less. It can be measured by adopts the following 2 methods:-

1. Survey Method

2. Study of Institutional Policies

1. **Survey Method :** Job discrimination may be ascertained by carrying out surveys in the industry or enterprise. During the surveys information about policies like recruitment, retrenchment, work conditions, conditions, promotion transfers, wages etc. are collected and conclusions are drawn.
2. **Study of Institutional Policies:** Another method to ascertain job discrimination is the study of Institutional Job Policies, such as :-
   (a) Hiring and Firing Recruitment Policies
   (b) Recruitment, Transfer, Promotion Policies
   (c) Training and Development Policies
   (d) Wage Policies, Fringe Benefits, Retirement Plans
   (e) Medical, Pregnancy and Disability Leave
   (f) Safety and Working Conditions Norms

Common Form of Job Discrimination Practices

Common forms of job discrimination:-

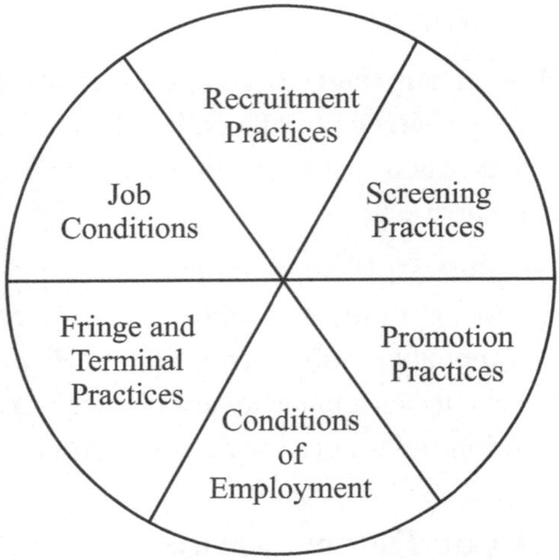

1. **Recruitment Practices:** Firms that solely rely on the word-of-mouth referrals of present employees o recruit new workers tend to recruit only from those social and sexual groups that are already represented in their labour force.
2. **Screening Practices:** Job qualifications are discriminatory when they are not relevant to the job to be performed (e.g. requiring a Ph.D or NET Qualification for post of Lecturer). Altitude or Intelligence Tests used to screen applicants become discriminatory when they serve to disqualify members from minority cultures who are unfamiliar with the language, concepts and social institutions used in the tests.

   Job Interviews are discriminatory of the interviewer routinely disqualifies women and minorities by relying sexual or racial stereotypes.
3. **Promotion Practices :** Promotion, job progression and transfer practices are discriminatory when the employees place males on job tracks separate from those open to women and minorities. When promotions rely on the subjective recommendations of immediate supervisors, promotion policy will be discriminatory.
4. **Conditions of Employment:** Wages and salaries are discriminatory to the extent that equal wages and salaries are not given to people who are doing essentially same work.

5. **Fringe and Terminal Benefit Practices:** If includes monetary and non-monetary benefits awarded to emplcyees along with pay. For example. A company may decide to allow conveyance allowance or medical facilities to executives only, may be considered as discriminatory.
6. **Job Conditions:** Job discrimination may also be an outcome of job conditions. The employers may create situations that may cause discrimination b/w employees. For Example, pressurizing female employees to work at late house, not allowing creche facility to children, not allowing break for the religious prayers or prohibiting maternity leaves etc. constitute discrimination on account of working conditions.

Dealing effectively with discrimination is a twofold process: become knowledgeable with regard to antidiscrimination laws, and pay close attention to what's happening in your company.

Here are some general guidelines for managers to follow then confronted by any type of discrimination:

- **Pay attention to what you don't always see.** You can't always see it, prove it, or stop it, but if you ignore even the hint of discriminatory behaviour, you and your company could suffer in the long run. Low morale, employee conflicts, and even lawsuits are just a few of the serious problems that could arise.
- **Don't play favorites.** If you offer certain benefits to employees, make sure these perks are available to everyone. For instance, it you want to provide a flexible work arrangement for your older workers, avoid appearing discriminatory by being sure to offer this option to everyone.
- **Keep your personal beliefs personal.** Your personal philosophy regarding race, religion, sexual orientation, and other potentially contentious issues should not affect your duty to monitor workplace discrimination, nor should it cloud your views regarding what's legal and just.
- **Be careful of what you say and to whom you say it.** It's easy for an off-the-cuff remark — said by either you or an employee — to start an avalanche of bad feelings and even a charge of discrimination. Think before you say something that might be misconstrued, and teach your employees to conduct themselves similarly. People should not be afraid to be themselves, but they do need to be careful, sensitive, and knowledgeable about what's okay to say and what's better left unsaid.

- **Respond quickly.** If an employee expresses concern about possible workplace discrimination, do what you can in the shortest period of time to resolve the issue. Allowing it to linger will only add to the employee's anxiety and allow whatever may be occurring to continue. Establish a clear policy for yourself and others for dealing with the problem. Do some intelligence gathering by having an honest conversation with the person who has lodged the complaint. Who said what? What exactly happened? Who else was involved? Along with the help and guidance of your human resources manager, talk to the person who has been accused. Make sure to take (and safeguard) copious notes of your discussions.
- **Educate yourself.** Stay informed about workplace discrimination. Talk with your peers in similar and different industries, read your daily newspaper for information about what's happening locally, and conduct research on discrimination and harassment law. Find out what it means for you as an employer. Consider paying an attorney who specializes in this area a one- or two-hour consulting fee, and ask as many questions as you can. Think of your investment as part of the cost of doing business. In the long-run, a short meeting could save you a lot of money.
- **Formalize the policy and the consequence.** Create and post an antidiscrimination policy (or consider paying an expert to create one). Keep in mind that no antidiscrimination policy will be taken seriously unless you take concrete action against any possible wrong doing. After you've assessed the situation and consulted a lawyer, determine how you're going to proceed. If you discover that some kind of discrimination has taken place, decide if you will start with a warning, insist on counseling, or formally terminate the accused.

Part - V

Social Responsibility of Business

- Corporate Social Responsibility
- Models of Management in Socio-Political Environment
- Public Policy of a Corporation and Its Role in a Market Society
- Total Ethical Management

24

Corporate Social Responsibility

INTRODUCTION

Business depends on the society for the needed inputs like money, men and skills. Business also depends on the society for market where products may be sold to their buyers. Thus, business depends on society for existence, sustenance and encouragement. Dependence of business on society is so complete that as long as that latter wants the former, business has reason to exist.

"Social responsibility is understood as the obligation of decision – markers to take actions which protect and improve the welfare of society as a whole along with their own interests."

Corporate Social Responsibilities

There are two basic approaches to the concept of **corporate social responsibility.**

Some theorists, focusing on the 'micro' level of analysis, try to show individual companies how **they can be more socially responsive**.

Other researchern concern themselves with the 'macro' level of analysis, assuming that the government, not individual companies, should establish a country's social goals.

Ackerman's Model: Micro-level theorist Robert Ackerman was among the earliest people to suggest responsiveness should be the goal of corporate social endeavour. Ackerman described three phases through which companies commonly tend to pass in developing a response to social issues.

In phase 1, a corporation's top managers learn of an existing social problem. At this stage, no one asks the company to deal with it. The chief executive acknowledges the problem by marking a written or oral statement of the company's policy towards it.

In phase 2, the company hires staff specialists or engages external consultants to study the problem and to suggest ways of dealing with it. Upto this point, the company has limited itself to declaring its intentions and formulating its plans.

Phase 3 is implementation. The company now integrate the policy into its ongoing operations unfortunately, implementation often comes slowly and often not until the government or public opinion forces the company to act. By that time, the company has lost the initiative. Ackerman thus advices that managers should "act early in the life cycle of any social issue in order to enjoy the largest amount of managerial discretion over the outcome."

Macro–level of social responsibility Four-stage model of corporate social responsibility

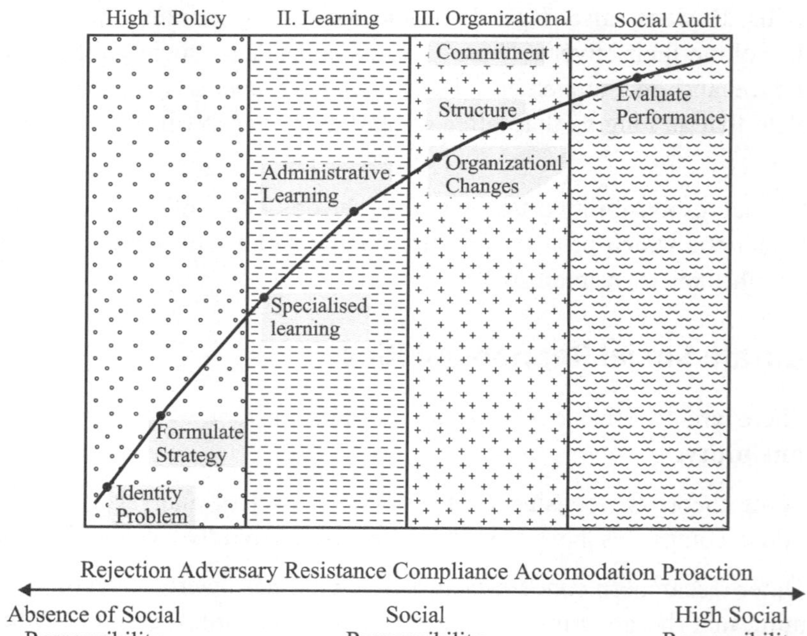

In the policy stage, the firm becomes aware of hose parts of the environment to which it needs to respond and action. Awareness may occur after stakeholder's expectations change, or it may result from an analysis of environment.

The firm needs to formulate on appropriable policy to respond to the society needs. The policy provides a framework for shaping other aspects of the organization's response. New production policies, for example, may result in better quality control, remove job hazards, and reduce water pollution.

There are six strategies towards corporate social responsibility.

First is **rejection**, a strategy in which a firm denies any responsibility for taking action on a social issue.

Second, is the **adversary strategy**, in which a firm fights to avoid having to take social actions but will, under severe pressure, cane in.

Resistance Strategy is third approach in which a firm may make token moves or act slowly to satisfy demands that it considers are beyond its social responsibilities.

Fourth is **compliance strategy**. In this posture, the firm simply decides to abide by a govt. request or a reasonable demand of some stakeholder group.

Fifth is the accommodation strategy in which a firm takes actions designed to address potential future stakeholder demands or other pressures, firms in this category do not oppose, strongly resist or out reluctantly.

Sixth is the proaction strategy in which a firm takes actions designed to address potential future stakeholder demands or other pressures.

Learning State

Specialised learning – Socio-technical expert–culture, life style's motivations etc.

Administrative learning – new routines that are necessary to cope with a social problem.

Organizational Commitment refers to the institutionalization of the new social policy by the firm.

Socio audit is a systematic study and evaluation of a firm's social performance.

Conclusion

Business is an organ of society and it operates in a socio-economic environment. It can justify its existence by fulfilling its obligations to the society. No doubt business is an economic institution and it cannot survive without economic performance. But economic results depend upon the goodwill and support of the society. Business can gain this support only when it assumes its social responsibilities.

AREAS OF CORPORATE SOCIAL RESPONSIBILITIES

Social responsibilities toward different stakeholders

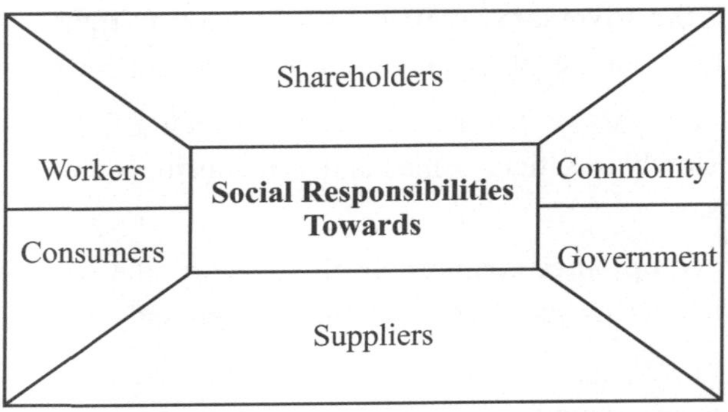

Introduction

The scope of social responsibilities of business is very wide. The responsibility is manifold and extends to all those who have a stake in business.

To be specific, the management of a business enterprise is responsible to:

(a) The inside group consisting of shareholders and employees, and

(b) The outside group consisting customer supplies, govt. and the community at large.

1. Shareholders

The just and foremost responsibility of business is to self i.e. to survive and grow. In non-corporate enterprises it implies responsibility to owners. In a company, shareholders are the legal owner, but they are entitled to appoint directors and regulate their activities.

Social responsibilities to shareholders or owners include:

(a) a fair and regular return on investment in the form of dividends.

(b) an adequate reward for the risk taken in the form of security and appreciation of capital so that the company can attract new capital from the market.

(c) Full and regular and accurate information on the progress and financial position of the company.

(d) Reasonable representation and participation of minority shareholders so as to ensure democratic management of corporate affairs.

This also includes responsibilities to debentureholders and other company.

2. Workers

The second group to which a business enterprise owes an obligation consists of those working in it. Such responsibility consist of:

(a) fair wage or salary for the contribution made.

(b) security of employment under proper and safe working condition.

(c) participation in decisions affecting their working life through union representatives.

(d) opportunity for personal advancement through education, training and experience.

(e) share in the increasing prosperity of business through bonus etc.

(f) meaningful work that provides job satisfaction, freedom and human treatment.

3. Consumers

Consumer is the foundation of business and satisfaction of consumer is the raison deter of business activities. This implies much more than the supply of goods and services. Unfair practices like hoarding, adulteration, shoddy merchandize, unfair measurement, misleading advertising etc. reveal that many business firms fail to fulfill their obligations to consumers:

(a) to supply goods of right quality at right time and place and at reasonable prices.

(b) to fit products to the needs and tastes of consumers of different classes and with different purchasing power.

(c) to inform and educate consumers on the arrival and use of new products.

(d) to be honest and truthful in the matter of advertising and warranty.

(e) to provide prompt, adequate and courteous after sale service to customers, and to handle their grievances property.

(f) to offer improved and new products through technical and marketing research.

(g) to avoid monopolistic and restrictive trade practices.

4. Suppliers

Every business concern owes an obligation to deal with its suppliers, dealers and competitors in a judicious manner. In order to develop healthy relations with suppliers, it is necessary to be honest and courteous with them. All dealings with supplies should be based on fair terms and conditions regarding prices, quality, delivery of goods, payment etc. undercutting and other unfair practices to exploit small and weak competitions should be avoided.

5. Government

Modern business is subject to several laws and regulations. If is the responsibility of management to conduct the affairs of the enterprise in accordance with the letter and spirit of law. Business must pay faxes and other dues to the govt. honestly, fully and promptly. In addition, business should help in establishing a democratic an socialistic society.

6. Community

Business is expected to act not only as an instrument of economic growth but also of social progress. Business must utilize the national resources efficiently and effectively for the satisfaction of society's weeds. As a good citizen, an enterprise should strengthen the culture and cohesion of the society. It is directly responsible for the development of local amenities in the town in which it functions. Every business firm is responsible for maintaining a healthy environment free from all types of pollution in the surrounding area. It can contribute to the well-being of local community by providing opportunities for employment, education, public health, housing etc. it can help society by providing them equal opportunities for growth. Business men fulfill their responsibility to community or the public when they so manage their firms as to make the public good the private good of the enterprise.

Reconciliation of Conflicting Claims

The above description reveals that business in responsible to several groups. The interests of these groups or stakeholders are not identical very often a conflict arises between them. Investors of a business want fair return, employees want regular employment at reasonable level of compensation, consumers want useful goods and services at the lowest possible price, govt.

wants the highest revenue and society wants a sensitive. As a result, management has to reconcile these conflicting demands. It has to act as an arbiter among. The various interests affected by business.

"Business Ethics and profit maximization are in contradiction" Comment?

Introduction

According to the classical economists, the role of business was to supply the goods and services desired the society through best possible utilization of available resources. Profit-maximize was considered to be the dominant goal of business. It has believed that the business of business is to be business and thus secure social and economic hands.

But, today, a business organization is not considered the sole prerogative of its owners but rather. The guardian of all those who have a stable in business.

Reasons for Profit Maximization and Business Ethics are in Contradictory

(i) Business is an economic institution

Business is an economic institution, and therefore, economic value is the sole criterion on by which the success of business should be measured. Profit is the barometer of an organization through the success and failure of the organization can be judged.

Ethics cost money and Business Ethics affect efficiency adversely. Being obliged to the employees, say a company runs its plant, even if it is incurring posses every year. Its efficiency goes down and its ability to compete is lost.

(1) A company which is inspired by ethical conduct is also profitable one

The driven companies are use to be successful the long-run, though in the short-run, they may lose money.

Are our Businessmen ethical? The answer with honourable exceptions is in the negative. It is too well known, most of our business men have lured by fast buck culture i.e. to earn as much money and as fast as possible. Ends justify the earns for our business men. It make health, you need it and the most better. But its why you exists.

(2) Better Environment for Business

Whether argument favouring social responsibility or Business ethics is that it creates a better environment. This concept rationalizes that a better society introduces environmental conditions more favoruable for business operations. They which is most responsive to the improve of community equality of life will as a result have a better community in which to conduct its business.

(3) Drucker, Friedman and Leviti's Views

The most cogent criticism has been voiced by the economist Milton Friedman. Friedman based his arguments on two principal contentions, one economical and one legal. From the economic respective, he asserted that if manager spend corporate funds on projects not intended to maximize profits, the efficiency of the market mechanism is to be undermined and resources will be his allotted within the economy. On the legal side, friedman contended that because managers are legal agents of the stockholders. Hence, if they had corporate funds for social purposes, they are entially stealing from the stockholders.

(4) Economic Efficiency should be the top priority of business

First and the most forceful argument disfavouring business ethics is that business has profit maximization as its main object. Infact, the business is most socially responsible when it attends its interests and leave other institutions.

Business's functions is economic, not social and economic values should be only criteria used to measure success. In this kind of system, managers have are agents of the stockholders, and all their decisions are controlled by their desire to maximize profits for the stockholders while reasonably complying with law and social custom.

(5) Ethics corresponds to basic human needs

It is a human trait that man desires to be ethical, not only in his private life but also in his business affairs, where, being, he knows his business may affect the lives of thousand of employees. Moreover, most people want to be part of an organization. Which they can respect and be publicly proud of because they perceive its purpose and activities to be honest and beneficial to the society. There is no inherent conflict between profit maximization and business ethics in the long-run. The realization of the profit maximization ultimately depends upon a favourable social responsibility by business that has to develop such an environment. It is shortsightedness to seek maximization of immediate profits at the cost of the very survival of business.

Business is an organ of society and it operates in a socio-economic environment. It can justify existence by fulfilling its obligations to the society.

No doubt business is an economic institution and it connot perform without economic performs. But economic performance results depend upon goodwill and support of the society. Business can gain the support and when it assumes Business Ethics.

Today, business enterprises are obliged to bear these social costs and internalise them in their operations.

In discharging business ethics, business should adopt a long-term view. It should not socially responsible actions merely because they reduce short-run profits.

The best example of this it TISCO which invests a lot (along with business ethics) to gain long-term profits, but can't rang to it, LIUON is the example which gained short-term profits with no social responsibility with regard to quality and quantity and price of the product.

Other examples are who have public and brand image in the market because they fulfilled the needs of the society are: Reliance, TATA, SONY, IBM etc.

25

Models of Management in Socio-Political Environment

There are 3 Models which aim at the enlistment of western industry and business.

I. The Chakraborty Model

II. The Jitatmananda Model

III. The Sherlekar Model

I. The Chakraborty Model

The model bases itself on Vedantic Concepts.

Vedanta is a systematic and formulated knowledge life and living. It helps to gain the knowledge of your Intrinsic self.

According to Chakraborty, there are 4 goals human system:-

1. **Dharma** (rectitude and righteousness)
2. **Artha** (money and wealth)
3. **Kama** (desires and needs)
4. **Moksha** (Liberation of spiritual ones)

The main features of Chakraborty model are:

1. To aim and strive for a "PURE MIND" — i.e. that is,
2. Work must be **done without personal claims** to egocentric results (rewards) as the primary driving force.

Desireless Results must by primary objective.

Work = Desireless Work (Nishkan Karma).

3. Balance is the keynote of Indian thought. It tries to maintain balance between short-term goals to material achievement and the ultimate divine protection.
4. Human personality complises:-
   a. An outer active, involved and dynamic self called "PRAKRITI".
   b. An inner quiescent witness and silent self called "PURUSHA".

To have an indepth awareness of the innerse self is crucial for effective self-management.

5. The credibility of a leader rests on the attribute of "**Impersonal Love**".
6. The Indian thoughts takes the Individual as a Contra Focus. It I am good, then the world is good.
7. No work is inferior or demeaning. Work is not any a means to gain name, fame or power but to purify our minds and ego and take is towards the attainment of bliss.
8. Knowledge is Indian thought speaks of 2 fundamental concepts:- CREATOR and CREATION. The Indian thought tries to seek knowledge about the creator rather the creation. The various Yogic Process, Social Norm and Values helps in transformation of minds to enable in establishing contact with the creator.

Thus, the model aims in ethico-moral transformation of both the worker and the manager.

In Chakraborty's news all these features can be summed up in context to Industry or Business in the "**Business Ashram**" vision which is as follows.

1. There should be a growing tendency towards products with longer life-cycles as against the shorter one today.
2. Organizations should tend to contract rather the expend as is the current tendency.
3. Localised, decentralized economic activities should include faster than centralized ones.
4. The need for high speed, long distance continuous travel should gradually decline. Bicycles should again come.
5. **Employee relations** should become more cooperative and less adversarial. **Spirit of Trusteeship** should also be implied amongst owner/top managers.
6. Competitive Advertising, making customers a prey must be reduced.
7. Business growth fuelled by greed and achieved through manipulations,

financial mergers and heavy debit financing should be favoured less.

8. The search for **strategic advantage**, **strategic intent, strategic response** or global market should be slowed down. Local resources for local markets to meet local needs should be the Principal Thrust.
9. Mental Illnesses due to overconsumption outside and undernourishment within should destine.
10. Loyalty and Gratitude to organization and colleague should become important features of professionalism.
11. Reduction in Greed and Interpersonal Rivalry should give way to basic human values like SHARING and HUMILITY.
12. **Networking** interpersonal or inter-organizational should be highlighted than the self-centered motive of survival.
13. Decision should be based on basic values of spirituality, ethics and ecologically positive or negative.
14. In education – Realization and Idealism should regain their lost importance as against the current trend of careerism.
15. Technology should be accepted or rejected by the standards set out by the spiritualised human being.
16. Alignment and Empowerment of the Individual will with the ultimate Divine will would lead to error-free morally correct decisions.
17. Finally, the workplace will tend to be transformed into a "spiritual/moral gymnasium". In this, the income profit etc. will be treated as a means of serving the basic physico-economic needs of employees and society.

Chakraborty stated that his model is Idealistic. The problems lies that when the ideals are set too high, instead of acting as an incentive, tends to act negatively as they can not be attainable.

The model also is silent about the visions and the objectives of an organization, which are central to ethical behaviours of a corporation and its management.

II. The Jitatmananda Model

Jitatmananda bases his model on the concept of practical Vedanta and particularly Swami Vivekananda.

The model rests on a few essential credos.

1. The Holistic Paradigm

According to the holistic paradigm two truths revolutionaries the body of management technique.

(a) A respectful athitude of honestly, help, care and encouragement are not only the beet policy but only poling in management.

(b) A worker can generate himself if empowerment, encourage trust, faith and support are offered to him.

Thus, holistic paradigm teaches:-

(i) Love begets love

(ii) Hatred begets hatred

(iii) Trust begets trust

(iv) Gratitude begets gratitude

(v) Respect begets respect

(vi) Empowerment begets responsible productivity

(vii) Meditation and spiritual practice provides guidance to corporate members

2. Creation of Ethical Leaders

(i) Whatever the excellent and best ones do, the commoness follow.

(ii) That leader is the best who has learnt the are of drawing different kinds o people towards him and extracting the best from each one according to his qualities and aptitude.

Factors which helps the leader to attract workers are:

(a) The workers must know that the leader sincerely feeds for them.

(b) The workers must see that the leader himself lanes to share all the works that the workers do.

(c) The workers must see that the leader practices what he preaches.

(d) The leader must be pure in body and mind.

(iii) The leader must lane the following essential qualities.

(a) Evenness or equanimity of mind. "Yoga Karma Kausalam Yoga" is skill in action.

(b) Capacity to face adverse situation with strength and calmness.

(c) Learn to be the servant to be able to rule.

(d) Ability to make the place of work a place of worship.

(e) Ability of creating the environment of a corporate family.

3. Creation of Self : Within as the source of all power. Four ways to manifest self-power are:-

(i) Knowledge

(ii) Devotion

(iii) Unselfish Action

(iv) Meditation

Meditation leads the leader through 7 levels of consciousness.

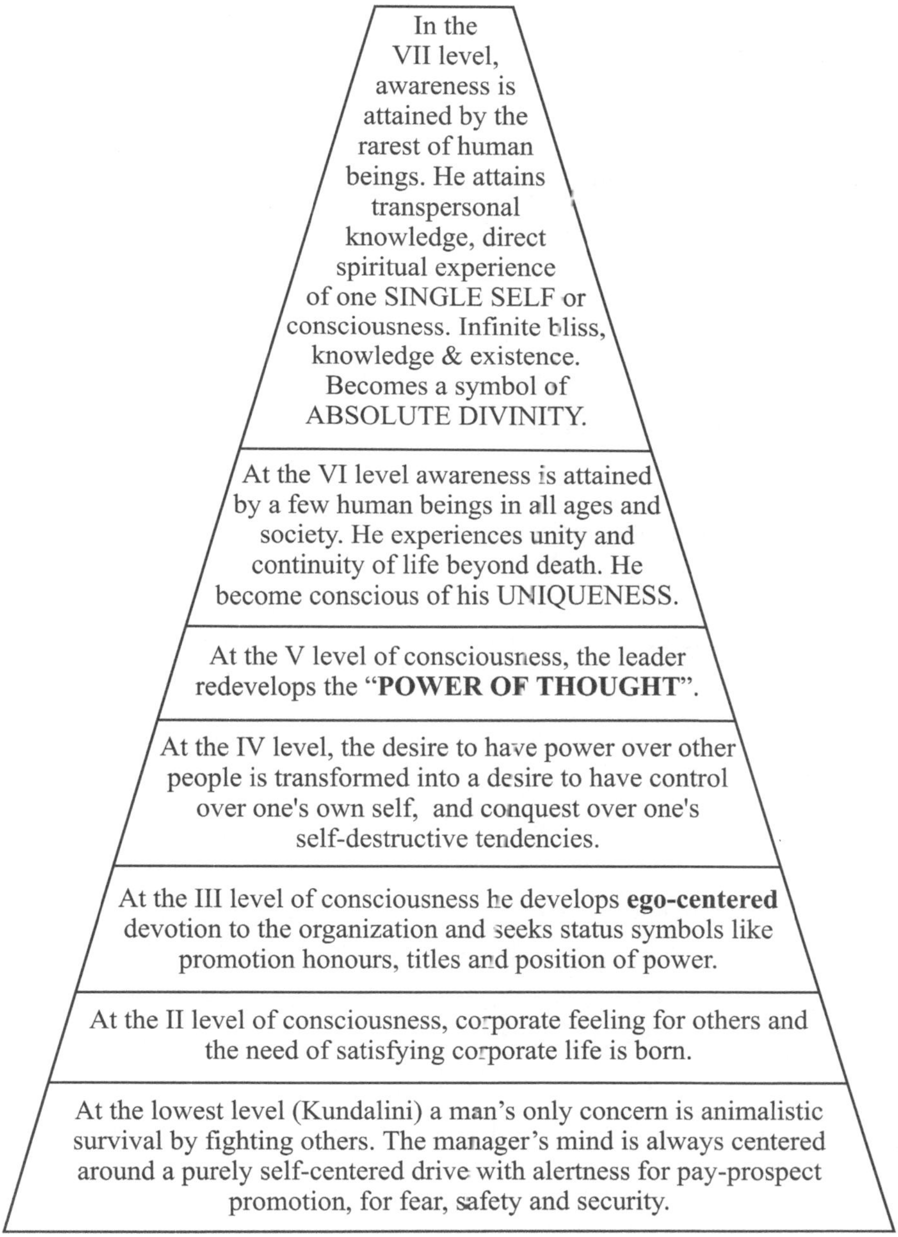

Seven Levels of Consciousness Attained by Meditation

4. Creative Leader Must Both Visionary and Missionary :

To create a leader of the highest creative power, four Qualities are necessary:

(a) The Yogi – a contemplative man, the quintessential thinker, who is fond of research, but finds it difficult execute his ideas into action.

(b) The Doer – who execute a plane or an idea efficiently, obediently without question.

(c) A visionary – with the power to envision.

(d) The capability to transform that vision and spiritual dynamism into others.

5. Company is a family- Vedic idea of a corporate culture.

Thus, the Jitatmananda model envisages the company culture to be entirely formulated around the leader-manager's culture.

The role of founder-entrepreneur or stockholder, his object vision are absent from the model.

III. The Sherlekar Model

The model is based on **turn ideals:**

(i) Human Values – spiritual, ethical and moral

(ii) Holism – unity, oneness, cooperation and synthesis

For the development of his thoughts, he depends upon certain Indian scriptures:

1. All work is an opportunity for doing good to the world and thus gaining materially and spiritually in on lives.
2. Worship people not only with the material things but also by showing respect to their ever-present divinity within.
3. Strength and inspiration for excelling in work comes from the Divine, God within, through prayer, hold readings and unselfish work.
4. He who works with calm and even mind achieves the most.
5. As we think, so we succeed, so we become. Attention to means ensures the ends.
6. By mutual cooperation, respect and fellow feeling, all of us will enjoy the highest good both material and spiritual.

7. Infinite happiness and infinite peace come to them who see the Divine in all beings.
8. Regal the other person as a divine being.

Based on these Indian Scripture's Principles, Sherlekar considers the following basic principles of Indian Ethos for Management:-

1. Immense potential energy and talents for perfection as human being has the spirit within his heart.
2. Karma Yoga offers double benefit of Private Benefit, self-purification and Public Benefit.
3. Excellence at work through self-motivation and self-development is the best means of Total Quality Mgmt.
4. Cooperation is a powerful instrument for term-work and success in any enterprise involving collective work.
5. Inner Qualities are much more powerful than the capital materials, plant and machinery which are outer resources.

Based upon the Sherlekar model the western management concepts and concepts based on Indian Ethos are following:-

Managerial Effectiveness Under / EM (Indian Ethos in Management)

The main job of management is not producing results. **Workers are to produce results; managers produce performers.**

Top management is Visionary. They plan 5 or 10 years ahead and performs 2 duties:-

1. To translate the vision or dream in terms of projects to be accomplished.
2. To develop performers who are self motivated. Worker's job to produce results by executing the projects.

S. No.	Item	Western Management	Management Based on Indian Ethos
1.	Belief	Production, productivity, profit at any cost.	Material gain, with belief in achieving human and social welfare also.
2.	Guidance	Management guided by mind only, led away by ego and desire. Soulless management.	Management by consciousness, power beyond mind, i.e., soul. Interiorised management.
3.	Emphasis	Worker development, management of others, profit maximization. Human being given only lip sympathy.	Development of man, Integrated growth, Harmony, happiness and health. Management of self.
4.	Tools	5 Ms as resources – men, money, materials, machines, markets. Science and technology. Information for decision marking.	Men, machines, materials and methods as conscious partners – all having consciousness whether manifested or dormant. Information and intuition for decision. Ethics and values combined with skills.
5.	Problem solving	Conflict resolution by negotiation, compromise, arbitration, liquidation of differences only for a temporary period. No reference to higher consciousness.	Conflict resolution through integration and synthesis on stressing super-ordinate common goals so that enduring harmony and unity is assured. Self introspection, stepping back aids the search for solution.
6.	Descision-making	Brain-storming (round table approach)	Brain-stilling (Entering the room of eternal silence).
7.	Development	Physical, vital and mental only. Soul or spirit ignored. Material development only, even at the cost of man and nature.	Integrated development, whole-man approach, breath control and meditation emphasized. Human enrichment and total quality.
8.	Approach	External behaviour. Mental, material, selfish only-soulless.	Noble attitudes.Inner guidance, team spirit, total harmony, global good.

Management Concepts

S. No.	Item	Current Definition	Definition as per Indian Ethos in Management
1.	Management	Getting things done.	Helping other people to produce extraordinary results.
2.	Productivity	Related to plant capacity.	Related to men's capability.
3.	Planning	Management by results.	Management by strategy
4.	Effective supervision	Concern for task and not for people.	Produce performers. Help the subordinates to develop leader ship qualities.
5.	Motivation of people	Maslow's theory of needs (some-times with some modification).	Emphasis on self-motivation by subordinates to develop leader ship qualities.
6.	Resources	Reliance almost on external resources.	Reliance almost on internal resources.
7.	Health of the company	Balance sheet and P/L account. Money oriented.	People oriented performance, environment friendly. Private as well as public benefit.
8.	Profitability	In terms of money. Social costs not included in balance sheet.	In terms of good public image. Social costs internalized.
9.	Hygiene factor	Attention only on job enrichment.	Primary emphasis on mind enrichment.
10.	Rights and duties	Emphasis on taking, not on giving. Rights become primary. Duties become subsidiary.	Emphasis on giving, not on taking. Duties given great importance and rights assume secondary values.
11.	Marketing	Keen competition to capture and retain demand: market driven economy.	Through cooperation by playing complementary role. Social awareness in marketing.
12.	System	Set of interrelated elements working as a whole. Hardware aspect. More emphasis on quantity and objective criteria.	Pattern of particular response expressed through organizational functioning. Software aspect. Equal emphasis on quality/ quantity with emphasis on subject aspect.

Cont.

S. No.	Item	Current Definition	Definition as per Indian Ethos in Management
13.	Structure	Hierarchical.	Organic, autonomous evolutionary.
14.	Growth	Ultimately dependent on turnover of goods.	Coordinating private and public benefit.
15.	Job Satisfaction	Hygiene factor. Creativity ignored.	Through innovation uniqueness, extraordinary results, trouble hooting.
16.	Training	Functional skills; not value oriented, or holistic.	Value oriented, holistic approach and equal emphasis on both (value/skills).
17.	Man-machine equation	Machine dominates man as human beings receive lip sympathy.	Man behind the machine given due regard. Healthy philosophy of life. Emotional stability.
18.	Man placement	As per qualifications and experiences.	More stress on natural inclination and character.
19.	Quality	Product by ISO, QM, QC. Human value, quality plays minor role. We have crises of values. Adulteration widespread.	Human quality; values, character, mind-enrichment. Wholeman approach. Mind and matter are given equal importance.

The Mind-set of a Manager

S. No.	According of Current Management Practices	S. No.	According to Indian Ethos in Management
1.	Produce results.	1.	Produce performers.
2.	Organise men, materials, machines and money	2.	Mobilise men and sound out other readiness.
3.	Plan, set goals, prepare schedules, checklists.	3.	Obtain agreement and commitment on means and ends.
4.	Motivate, praise, reprimand, punish, push people.	4.	Inspire, empower, celebrate success, mourn failure, draw people.
5.	Check, control, report at command post.	5.	Set personal example, visible, accessible, on the move.
6.	Coordinate, requisition, convene meetings.	6.	Facilitate, show ways to overcome.
7.	Instruct, issue notices, order, demand compliance.	7.	Make queries, sound out ideas, encourage suggestions.

Thus, Sherlekar model is based on Indian Ethos in Management.

He emphasises on the core character or role player that is the Manager. Accordingly, he defines and compares it with western concepts, the role of a manage, their characteristics major activities, quality mindset and major jobs.

Thus, Sherlekar model gives a much more clearer idea of the manager and the model is more effective with regard to implementation and monitoring of the model.

CONCLUSION

To summaries the 3 models, following points can be drawn:

(a) In more of the 3 models, the organization, its object or mission gets any attention.

(b) All 3 models implicitly accepts profit measurements and creation of competitive advantage as the basic objective of an organization.

(c) Neither Chakraborty, nor Swami Jitatmananda Model nor Sherlekar have made any reference to or suggested total or partial implementation of their models.

26

Public Policy of a Corporation and Its Role in a Market Society

The business institution has been reshaped and the managerial role affected by many public policy measures designed to accomplish both economic and non-economic goals and objectives of the larger society.

Public Policy can be defined as a specific course of action taken by society by a legitimate representative of society addressing a specific problem of public concern that reflects the interests of society or particular segments of society.

This definition emphasizes a course of action rather than discrete actions taken with respect to particular problems: it does not restrict such action to government, and does not claim that each and every public policy represents the interests of society as a whole. Enough interests have to be represented so that the policy is supported and can be implemented effectively.

The **public policy agenda is that collection of topics** and **issues** with respect to which public policy may be formulated.

There are many problems and concerns that a people in society would like to see acted upon but on those that are important receive attention from policy makers complies the public policy agenda.

Such an agenda is found in the collective judgment of society, actions and concerns of interest groups, legislations introduced into parliament, cases being considered by the supreme court etc.

The manner in which problems in our society get on the public policy agenda is complex and involves many different kinds of political participation.

The specific course of action that is eventually taken with respect to a problem is decided through the *public policy process.*

The term public policy process **refers to the various processes by which public policy** is formulated. It is made by means of a complex, subtle and not always formal process.

The formulation of public policy is not limited to formal acts of government but can be achieved by interest groups that bring issues to public attention and attempt to influence public opinion as well as business and government.

The policies are formed through a process involving, **public opinion, interest groups, institution, media** etc.

Public policy can be made through legislation passed by the parliament, regulations issued by government agencies or decisions handed down by the Supreme Court.

The process of making public policy begins in the society as problems and issues are defined, then issues find formal way for policy decisions through institutions and then return to society for implementation.

Elements of the Public Policy Process

The public policy process can be broken into various elements:

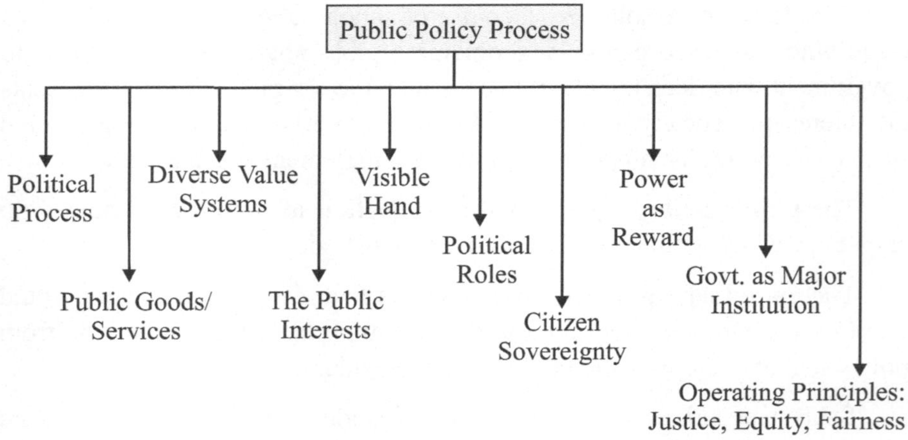

I. Political Process

The values are assigned to particular entity in the public policy process and decisions are made about the allocation of resources through a political process. It is a complex amalgam of power and influence that involves may people pursuing different interests who try to persuade and influence other people in order to achieve their objectives.

However, it is difficult to determine who has the most power and influence in this process.

Polities is also called as the art of the possible, which means that a balancing of interests is necessary to resolve conflicts between interests in order to arrive at a common course of action.

The outcome of political process reflects the principle that no one gets everything they want and get everyone has to get something in order to be satisfied that the objective is worth pursuing.

Compromise and Negotiation are necessary skills to participate effectively in the political process.

The function of a political process is to organize individual effort to achieve some kind of social goal or objective.

The task of political system is to adjudicate such conflicts by:

(a) Establishing rules of the game for participants in the system.

(b) Arranging compromises and balancing interests of various participants.

(c) Enacting compromises in the form of public policy measures.

(d) Enforcing these public policies.

The outcome of political process is not usually under the control of a single individual or group, as is the outcome of an exchange process. The outcome depends on how much power and influence one has, how skillful one is at compromising and negotiating and the variety and strength of other interests involved.

Decisions can be made by vote where the majority rules, by building a consensus, or by excursing raw power and coercing other members of a group to agree with your causes of action.

For example. The outcome of the exchange process is certain as people usually know that their decisions are directly connected to the outcome. If people choose to part with a sum of money, they only do so because they know they will receive a product or service they want in return. Produces sell their products for a specific sum of money not for some promise to pay an unspecified amount.

However, the value of goods and services as well s money changes over time but the public is aware of what they are getting unless some frond is involved.

II. Public Goods and Services

The reason public policy decisions have to be made trough a political process is the nature o the goods and services that are provided through the public policy process.

Public goods and services implies that no one own these goods and services invidually - *they are collectively owned* or *held in common* and *private property rights do not apply.*

Public goods and services are indivisible i.e. the quantity produced cannot be divided into individual units to be purchased by people according to their individual preferences. For emample, one cannot buy a piece of clean air to carry around and breath wherever one goes.

Nor can one buy a share of national defence over which one would have control.

Thus, this indivisibility gives these goods and services their public character because if people are to have public goods and services at all, they must enjoy roughly the same amount.

As goods are indivisible among large number of people the society must register its desice for public goods and services through the political process. It is only through the political process that compromises can be reached that will resolve the value conflicts.

III. Diverse Value System

Because of the existence of diverse value systems value conflicts are more pronounced in the public policy process.

These is no underlying value system into which other values can be translated, no common denominator by which to assess trade-off's and make decisions about resource allocation to attain some common economic objective as improving one's material standard of living or increasing the nation's gross national product.

The overall objective of clean air and water, equal opportunity, occupational safety and health and other public goods and services is meant to improve the quality of life for all members of society.

For Example : the cost of pollution – control equipment can be determined in economic terms. The benefits this equipment provides should be positive in improving health by reducing the amount of harmful pollutants people has to breathe and improving the aesthetic diversion by making clear air.

The difficulty is analysed through following questions what is the price tag for the lives saved by avoiding future diseases that may be caused by pollution? What is the value of reducing the probability that children will be born with abnormalities because of toxic substances in the environment? What is the value of preserving one's heaving because money has been spent to reduce the noise emitted by machinery in the workplace?

The difficulty of expressing all these intangibles economic terms so that people's preferences are matched should be apparent.

There are atleast 5 ways of determining the value of a human life:

(a) Calculating the present value of estimated future earnings that are foregone due to premature death.

(b) Calculating the present value of the losses others experience because of a person's death.

(c) Examining the value placed on an individual life by presently established social policies and practices.

(d) Using the 'willingness to pay' method where people are asked how much they would be willing to pay to reduce the probability of their death by a certain amount.

(e) Booking at the compensation people accept as wage premiums for dangerous jobs or hazardous occupations.

IV. The Public Interest

The universal motivating principle in the public policy process is the public interest rather than self-interest. This principle is invokes by those who make decisions about public policy. Elected public officials claim to act in the interest of the nation or state as a whole. The public interest group claim to be devoted to **general or national welfare.**

The term *Public Interest* have 4 meanings:

1. It refers to the aggregation, weighing and balancing a number of special interest. It results through the free and open competition of interested parties who have to compromise their differences to arrive at a common course of action. It is the *sum total of all private interests in the community that all balanced for the common good.*
2. It can also refer to a **common or universal interest that all or at least most of the members** of a society share. A decision is in the **public interest** if it serves the **ends of the whole public.** It assumes a great deal of commonality as to basis wants and needs of the people who comprise a society.
3. An idealist perspective is that it judges alternative courses of action in relation to some absolute standard of value, which may exist independently of individual preferences. The public interest is not only more than the sum of private interests, it is something distinct and apart from basic needs and wants of human beings. The difficulty is finding someone with a godlike character.
4. Public interest focuses on the process by which decisions are made rather than the specification of some ideal outcome. This definition involves the acceptance of some process, as majority rule, to resolve differences among people.

Politicians want to get reelected and will note for those goods and services they believe have an appeal to the majority of their constituency. Public Interest Groups want to extend their power and influence in society and are called Special Interest Groups. Thus, the definition of Public Interest can never be entirely divorced from the self-interest of those who are making decision.

V. The Visible Hand

The resources are allocated in the public policy process by a visible hand. The visible hand is the **group of decision makers** in the public policy process who have been most active and influential in arriving at a common course of action.

They consciously allocate resources and it they make wrong and do not adequately serve the public interest they can be held accountable and removed from their position of power and influence.

The decisions about resource allocation are visible in the certain people in public policy process — elected public officials, govt. bureaucrats, public interest group — all can be held accountable for there decisions if they are not in public interest and thus not acceptable throughout entire society.

VI. Political Roles

People play different roles in the public policy process. These roles have a political character.

Elected public official are directly involved in the public policy process.

They have an influence on public policy outcomes. They are the key decision-makers in the public policy matters / process and have most visible impact on the outcome of the public policy process.

The average person simply plays the role of citizen by voting for a representative of his or her choice, contributing money to a campaign, writing elected public official on particular issues and similar measures.

Joining large social movements are another way for average person to exercise political influence.

VII. Citizen Sovereignty

Citizens are considered as sovereign over the public policy process as consumers are sovereign over the market system.

The citizens as consumers are sovereign as they have **Vote**, which is the ultimate power that citizens have in a democratic systems.

A public official can be voted out of office if he or she does not perform as the majority of citizens in his or her constituency. The citizens cab vote someone else into office whom they believe will make decisions about allocation of resources for production of public goods and services that are more consistent with the citizens preferences as a whole.

The citizens cab express their preferences and try to influence the outcome of the public policy process either individually through contact with public officials or collectively through interest groups.

There are 2 ethics related problems/issues that concern the citizen sovereignity:

1. One concerns with the **idea of manipulation** relates to the candidates for elected public office who are advertised and packaged as a product by using the medium of T.V. advertising, which is used more and more in political campaigns. The citizens are manipulated by there promotions techniques and vote for an image created by the television advertising rather than for an individual whom they do know.
2. Second problem is the **bad reputation** that the average citizen has with regard to the **participation in the political process.** Voter

turnouts are very low in the election. Most of those who do vote probably know little about the candidates and issues that are at stake in the elections. People who do not participate in public affairs sacrifice their sovereignty and power to minority in the society.

VIII. Power as Reward

The reward for a public official or candidate for office is the attainment of **power** and influence in the public policy process.

Power is the lifeblood of politicians, without which they will wither and die.

If an incumbent has done a good job and supplied public goods and services to the citizens, he may be reelected than an official who does not fulfill public demands.

IX. Government as the Major Institution

The major institutional force operative in the public policy process is the government, primarily the Democratic government, then the state or local govts. Other institutions which are also active in the public policy process are:

(a) **Business** has been an institutional force in the public policy process.

(b) **Public Interest Groups** are also influential in the public policy process.

But, **Government** is the principal institution involved in formulating public policy that shapes the behaviour of business organizations. It is the **Government** which legitimizes the policies and convert them into public policy for adoption, implementation and enforcement.

Government policies have a wider scope than the business policies which are fromed for a particular segment of the society.

X. Operating Principles

The operating principle of the public policy process are : **Justice, Equity and Fairness.**

These are invoked to justify the decisions made in the public policy process about resource allocation.

The government to establish there operating principles involves itself in a complex process of Negotiation and Compromise and divides Authority and applies checks and balances to limit power.

27

Total Ethical Management

Total Ethical Management is a description of the culture, attitude and organization of a company that strives to provide customers with products and services that satisfy their needs.

The term TEM (Total Ethical Management) indicates:

Total : Total refers the total personality, characteristics attitude, sincerity, actions and behaviour. It means the involvement of total human being and his character.

Ethic : Ethics involves learning what is right or wrong, and then doing the right things. Business Ethics relates to what is right or wrong in the workplace and doing what's right with regard to effects of products / services and relationships with the stakeholders.

Management : Mgmt. is a process of managing the mind, directing the behaviour and assessment and development of skills which a total human being is serving the society in a right manner.

Total Ethical Management (TEM) : It is a philosophy the involves everyone in an organization in a continual effort to improve quality and achieve customer satisfaction.

The four principles of an Highly Ethical Organization :

1. They are **obsessed with fairness.** They believe that other person's interests counts more than their own.
2. They see their activities in terms of purpose. The purpose ties the organization to its environment.
3. There exists a clear vision and picture of integrity throughout the organizaiton.

The total ethical management tries to adopt there principles. Such a organization understands that every significant management decision has ethical value dimension. Everyone is expected to work through conflicting stakeholder value perspectives.

The Eight Elements of TEM

To be successful in implementing TEM, an organization must concentrate on the following 8 key elements of ethics :

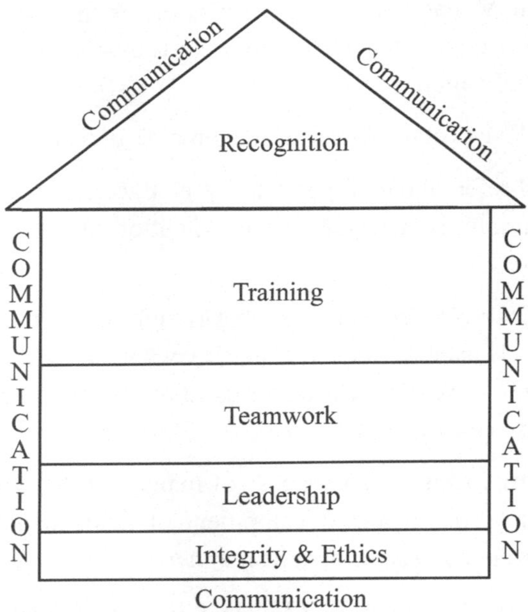

Total Ethical Management (TEM) has been coined to describe of philosophy that makes quality the driving force behind Leadership, Design, Planning, and Improvement Initiatives.

For this Total Ethical Management requires the help of the following 8 key elements:

1. Ethics
2. Integrity
3. Trust
4. Training
5. Teamwork
6. Leadership
7. Recognition
8. Communication

These elements cab be divided into 4 groups according to their function for making organizations total ethics

I. Foundation : It includes Ethics, Integrity and Trust
II. Building Bricks : It includes Training, Teamwork and Leadership
III. Binding Mortar : It includes Communication
IV. Roof : It includes Recognition.

I. Foundation

Total Ethical Management is built on the foundation of Ethics, Integrity and Trust. It fosters openness, fairness and sincerity and allows involvement of everyone.

1. **Ethics :** is the discipline concerned with good and has in any situation. It includes Individual Ethics and Organizational Ethics. The Individual Ethics include personal rights and wrongs.

   Organizational Ethics establish a business code of ethics that outlines guidelines that all employees are to adhere to in the performance of their work.

2. **Integrity:** implies honesty morals, values, fairness and adherence to the facts and sincerity. The characteristic is what customers (internal or external) expect and deserve to receive. TEM will not work in an atmosphere of duplicity.

3. **Trust :** Trust is a by-product of integrity and of TEM cannot be built. It fosters full participation of all members. It encourages commitment, allows decision making at appropriate levels in the organization, helps to ensure that measurements focus on improvement of process and are not used to contend people. Trust builds the cooperative environment

essential for the TEM. Trust is essential for ensuring **Customer Satisfaction.**

II. Bricks

Basing on strong **foundation** of Trust, Ethics and Integrity, bricks are placed to reach the roof **Recognition**.

It includes:

4. **Training :** is very important for employees to be highly productive. Supervisors are solely responsible for implement the **TEM** within their departments, and teaching their employees the philosophies of **TEM**. Various areas in which employees need training are "interpersonal skill, the ability to function within teams, problem solving, decision making, job mgmt. performance analysis and improvement, business economics and technical skills." During the creation and formation of TEM employees are trained so that they become effective employee of the company.
5. **Teamwork :** To be successful in business, teamwork is also important element of TEM. With the use of teams, the business will receive quicker and better solutions to problems. Teams also provide more permanent improvements in processes and operations. In teams, people feel more comfortable bringing up problems that may occur, and can get help from other workers to final a solution and put into place. There are 3 types of teams that TEM organizations adopt:
   - **(a) Quality Improvement Teams or Excellence Teams (QTIS):** These are temporary teams with the purpose of dealing with specific problems that often re-occur. These teams are set up for a period of **three to twelve months.**
   - **(b) Problem Solving Teams (PST) :** These are temporary work teams to solve certain problems and also to identify and overcome causes of problems. They generally lost from one week to there months.
   - **(c) Natural Work Teams (NWT) :** These teams consist of small groups of skilled workers as employee involvement teams, self-managing teams and quality circles. These teams generally work for one to two hours a week.
6. **Leadership:** is the most important elements in TEM, and appears everywhere in organization. It requires the manager to provide an **inspiring vision**, make **strategic directions** that are understood by

all and to **instill values** that guide subordinates. For successful **TEM**, the supervisor must be committed in leading his employees. A supervisor must understand and believe in ethics and demonstrate their **belief** and **commitment** through their daily practices of TEM. The leader makes sure that the strategies philosophies, values and goals are transmitted down they out the organization to provide **Focus Clarity** and **Direction.**

A key point is that TEM has to be introduced and led by Top Management through their commitment and Personal Involvement is creating and deploying clear quality values and goals, consistent with the objectives of the company.

III. Binding Mortar

7. **Communication:** Communication binds everything together. It acts as a vital link between all the elements of TEM. It means a common understanding of ideas between the sender and the receiver.

   The success of TEM demands communication with and among all the organization members, suppliers and customers.

   For the communication to be credible the message must be clear and receives must interpret in the way sender intended.

IV. Roof

8. **Recognition :** Recognition is the last and find element in the entire TEM system.

   It should be provided for both suggestions and achievement for teams as well as individuals.

   Employees strives to receive recognition for themselves and their teams.

   In a TEM, when people are recognized, there are huge changes in self-esteem, productivity, quality and the amount of effort exhorted to the task at hand.

   Also, in a TEM system recognition is important to be given immediately following an action that an employee has performed.

Conclusion

Thus, there elements are key in ensuring the success of TEM in an organization and without these the business entities cannot be successful TEM implements.

Part - VI

Contemporary Ethical Issues

- Spirituality in the Workplace
- Indian Ethos for Management
- Vedanta and Managers
- Indian Heritage in Production and Consumption
- Personal Growth and Lessons from Ancient Educational System
- Total Quality Management: An Indian Insight

28

Spirituality in the Workplace

Management has become an essential feature of everyday life **at home**, **in the office or factory** and in **government**. In all types of organization, where a group of people assemble or a common purpose, management principles come into play trough the management of resources, finance and planning, policies and procedures.

In the field of management, there has been an uprising of the term '**Spirituality**' in management or workplace.

According to the Management Gurus, basically there are 2 reasons for this increased interest in spirituality: -

1. **The need of employees for meaningful existence**. This lies that spirituality is required people not only in their personal but also in their professional life.
2. The corporate Leadership is looking for new ways to motivate employees and create innovative solutions.

MEANING OF SPIRITUALITY

According to Oxford Advanced Learner's Dictionary the word '**Spirituality**' means "state as quality of being concerned with spiritual matters."

However, there are different interpretations of the work by different people.

- Some associate it with God
- While some others consider it as a state of mental place and happiness.

In clear terms **spirituality** is a process to develop the sense of morality and ethics within oneself which helps the individual to be stable and correct during the interpersonal transactions.

Workplace Spirituality

Different companies define spirituality in the workplace differently.

Some companies consider spirituality as:-

1. Bringing values to work and using them in everyday life. Individual values such as **honesty, integrity** and **good quality work.**
2. **Treating each customer, employee** and **co-worker** with **respect** and **love**.
3. For some companies spirituality is **using Prayers, Meditation**, in making all the small and large **decisions** each day.
4. Being socially responsible for the community, environment and the world. They see their companies serving the **3 'P' People, Planet** and **Profit**.
5. Certain companies are embracing Key Spiritual Values embraced in a business context as **integrity, honestly, quality accountability, cooperation, service, intuition, trustworthiness, respect and justice**.
6. Certain companies believe that spiritual workplace is place beyond earning our daily bread. It is a place where the whole person can express themselves.
7. Some corporate business consider Cr**eativity** as the core of the business. To realize this goal we must create environments where spirit flourishes. When people incorporate spirituality they work more efficiently as teams for they are living values that nurture others. If leadership is exercised based on spiritual values, then **character** and **reputation** are built which are required for the growth.

Seven Principles of Spirituality in the Workplace

Spirituality in the workplace can be defines using seven principles:

1. Creativity
2. Communication

3. Respect
4. Vision
5. Partnership
6. Energy
7. Flexibility

All the seven principles are related to each other and are important.

Spirituality has no religious component or preference, but it is a way of expressing humanity.

1. Spirituality is Creativity

Creativity includes the use of colour, taught and freedom to enhance productivity.

Creativity is fun. When people enjoy what do, they work much harder.

Creativity includes conscious efforts to see things differently, to break out of habits and out-dated beliefs to find new ways of thinking, doing and being.

It is a natural, normal aspect of human beings.

Suppression of **creativity** leads to violence. When they are forced to crush their creativity, its energy force turns to destructive release.

So, Creativity as a principle of spirituality is a must.

2. Spirituality is Communication

Communication is a vehicle that allows people to work together.

In our society, our learning process is based on learning to communicate with everyone.

Through the **communication** process we try to win the favour of the 'parent', 'teacher' or 'adult' and try not to get punished.

Learning to listen to others, really hear them, speak the truth and **come together** in human understandings leads to powerful productivity for all involved.

Both in **personal relationship** and in **work relationship** good communication skills are most important to generate spiritunation in the organization.

Lack of **communication** leads to **isolation, confusion, conflict, unnecessary anxiety, mistrust and suspicion.**

3. Spirituality is Respect

Respect of **self** and of **others**: respect for the environment; other people's personal privacy, their physics space and belongings; different viewpoints, philosophies, religion, gender lifestyle; ethnic origin, physical ability, belief and personality.

Along with Respect comes **Acceptance**, which includes acceptance of the inherent right of each person to follow their chosen life path and acceptance that directing and variety lead to a rich mixture of humanity.

Lack of respect and acceptance leads to conflict and hostility.

4. Spirituality is Vision

Vision means seeing beyond the obvious-seeing the unseen. It is a common trait, used to describe the leaders and entrepreneurs.

For some people **vision** is an inborn trait. They see a **vision** of what can be, of the various possibilities and then head straight to achieve it, overcoming all obstacles.

Vision can be learned. The only requirement is strong desire to want to learn, coupled with strong desire to grow and expand beyond where you are.

Vision can grow only when there is workplace spirituality. When people are happy at workplace and where people get opportunity to be creative.

5. Spirituality is Partnership

Partnership encompasses **individual responsibility** and **trust** that other people will perform according their commitment for the good of team and partners.

Partnership accepts that different people have different dewponds and beliefs; these differences are used as **positive aspects** or building team experience.

Partnership encourages a balanced and fair way of being and working together, as well as honest disagreement without hostility or warfare.

Partnership encourages the gender equality, without over-ruling or dominating each other.

Lack of Partnership leads to isolation and unhealthy competition.

So the corporate culture must have partnership to develop workplace spirituality.

6. Spirituality is Energy

Positive energy forces are released when people feel creative, when people have the freedom to express their opinions, and when people feel respect from their management and their press.

Workplace spirituality can be created by the positive energy i.e. (1) contribution to the collective positive energy using their own creativity, by (2) communicating will, be (3) having respect for others, by (4) adapting to changing situations, by (5) working well with others and by (6) enjoying what you do.

Collective negative energy is—withholding your talent, communicating without respect, fighting and arguing with others, resisting changes, creating tension with others and hating what you do.

7. Spirituality is Flexibility

Flexibility includes the ability to adapt to the changing situations and allowing one's own beliefs and habits to changes as needed.

Learning **to see trends** and **prepare for them** is one way of learning **flexibility.**

Another way is to learn about our strengths and weaknesses.

Learning new concepts leads to spirituality.

Apart from these:

Spirituality also implies

- Fun
- Finding yourself

Spirituality is Fun

People who enjoy their life work harder, make more money, have more confidence in themselves, have more friends. By doing so, one can work in more better way, free from stress which would lead to spirituality or fun at workplace.

Spirituality is Finding yourself

Learning about who are, how you can control your world by changing your attitude, and learning to **respect** and **accept** others helps units us together.

Thus, to conclude **spiritualism at workplace is:**

1. Not compromising your personal set of values / ethics or personal happiness.
2. Keeping the balance in your life.
3. Going with the flow, rather than fighting every inch of the way.
4. Having a mind like water.
5. Feeling fulfilled in what you do.
6. A way to express the divine in your work.
7. Doing work that brings you personal happiness.

Benefits / Importance of Spirituality in Workplace

Spiritual workplace means that work would move from merely being a place to get energy money to survive from just earning our daily bread – to being a place of livelihood.

There are various benefits of a spiritual workplace:

1. One of the primary benefits is that people all more in touch with the **source of creativity**. Creativity is a cornerstone of business as it allows us to come out with new products and services to or generate new ideas that really are of service. Creativity leads to more efficient contribution. Spirituality leads to create an atmosphere is which **creativity and innovation** flourish.
2. Another benefit is increased authenticity in communication. As spirituality is communication, it helps to create a "**safe space**" i.e. in which people feel free to talk about their truth without fear of reprisal. Through the spirituality, old problems clear up, new possibilities emerge, people feel more aligned and they work in a **trusting team**.
3. Spirituality gives rise to Teamwork, Cooperation, Trust and Collaboration. When people are provided to work in an atmosphere where there is no selfish feelings then people work in a Team. This culture can be developed through spiritualism.
4. Increased Ethical and Moral Behaviour is get another benefit of spirituality in the workplace. Through the development of **mutual trust, respect and acceptance** spirituality cab emerge which in turn, gives birth to the inculcation of ethical and moral behaviour among the employees. Employees trust employers, employers trust employees and customers trust a company's and remain loyal for lifetime.

29

Indian Ethos for Management

Management has become part and parcel of our life. Every individual and group is managing its different tasks towards the goal and target. Management is a systematic way of performing all activities in field of human effort. It is about keeping oneself engaged in interactive relationship with other human being in the course of performing one's duty. According to Peter Orucker- "It is the task to make people capable of joint performance to make their witness irrelevant."

Ancient Indian thoughts and principles are based holy book Gita and Upanishad. Basic principles of Indian Wisdom are:

- Nishkam Karma
- Work is worship
- Propkar punyay, papaya parpidnam (it is virtue to help other and sin to harass others)

So, the whole world should be treated as friends.

"Vasudhaiva Kutumbkam"

From ancient time Indian culture is based on academic culture. Our personal and professional life is guided by these ethics and values. Since it is the age of globalization, the whole world is coming closer day-by-day.

Management Guidelines from The Bhagavad-Gita

There is an important distinction between effectiveness and efficiency in managing. Effectiveness is doing the right things and efficiency is doing things right.

The general principal of effective management can be applied in every field of life. The difference may be mainly in the application than in principles. Again effective management is not limited in its application for only to business or industrial enterprises but to all organization where the aim is to reach a given goal through a chief executive or a manager with the help of a group of workers.

The manager's functions can be briefly summed up as under:

- Forming a vision and planning the strategy to realize such vision.
- Cultivating the art of leadership.
- Establishing the institutional excellence and building an innovative organization.
- Developing human resources.
- Teambuilding and teamwork.
- Delegation, motivation, and communication.
- Reviewing performance and taking corrective action whenever required.

Thus management is a process in search of excellence to align people and get them committed to work for a common goal to the maximum social benefit.

The critical question in every manager's mind is how to be effective in his job. The answer to this fundamental question is found in the Bhagavad-Gita, which repeatedly proclaims that you try to manage yourself. The reason is that unless the manager reaches a level of excellence and effectiveness that sets him apart from the others whom he is managing, he will remain be merely a teamhead in the crowd and not an achiever.

In this context the Bhagavad-Gita, expounded thousands of years ago by the super management guru Lord Sri Krishna, enlightens us all managerial techniques leading to a harmonious and blissful state of affairs. These activities are performed against conflict, tension, lowest efficiency and least productivity, absence of motivation and lack of work culture etc. common to most of the enterprises today.

The modern management concepts like vision, leadership, motivation, excellence in work, achieving goals, meaning of work, attitude towards work, nature of individual, decision making, planning etc., are all discussed in the Bhagavad-Gita with a sharp insight and finest analysis, making it highly eligible to become part of the modern management syllabus.

Why Indian Ethos in Management

1. To have an appropriate management style
2. To show how ethical value help in management
3. To show how a person should be great achiever with peaceful life.

Principle of Management as per Indian Wisdom described in Gita and Upanishad

Indian ethos for management refers to the application of principle of management as per Indian wisdom described in Gita and Upanishad. These principles are:

1. **Each soul is a potential God:** Every human being is a part and particle of the almighty God. His heart and soul is directly attached to the divine power. Therefore every human being has adequate power and energy for his self-development. He can do anything and everything if his efforts are for common good and excellence and God always helps people for their development. Here human power is more important than industrial capacity and productivity.
2. **Holistic Approach:** Holistic approach of management refers the whole world is a union. All the people are same. There is no difference between them given from God. This is a concept of Advaita. So, the management should not make any difference or discrimination on the basis of religion, caste, society or culture. All people should be given equal opportunity to develop and prove themselves. The organization should make collective work with the effort of all people. It will give harmonious and peaceful life.
3. **Equal importance to subjectivity and objectivity:** Indian Ethos of management combines both subjective and objective resources. Subjective resources refer to ethical values and qualities as - integrity, purity, truth, social awareness, courage, vision etc., which are related to our heart and soul. Objective resource refer to materialistic things as

-money, material, machine, information etc. If we combine these qualities and resources, there will be much development in our internal and external life. This will give total quality of mind as well as total quality of material. So, we should open our insight vision to achieve these things.

4. **Karma Yoga (Selfless Work) or Niskam Karma:** Human life is made to work. But this work should no be only for self. Karma yoga refers to selfless service to other. We should work for other, for society, for nation. With development of society and nation, we will also develop. We should do our best and with our active participation. We should be devoted to our work. Only this work will give us the way to serve the society and ourselves.

5. **Yogah Karmasu Kaushalam (Excellence of Work):** Yogah refers to concentration for excellence. Every work should be excellent. We should work with determination and ability. It will results in a smart work. Our head, heart and soul should cooperate with our hand. It will give us the qualities of wisdom worker.

6. **Co-operation:** Co-operation refers to the collect or teamwork. In this modern life, there is too much competition for survival and growth. But, the cut-throat competition is not good for anyone, it will give nothing. Only healthy competition will provide services for social and common good. By mutual help and cooperation we can achieve the heights of human welfare and development and this will lead a harmonious and peaceful life.

Essential Features of Indian Ethos and Insights

1. The divinity of human being is not an idea but a truth. It can be felt in calm mind.
2. Balance or equilibrium is stable state of Indian thought i.e. balance between desire and desirelessness, spiritual and secular values. Subjective and materialistic world.
3. Indian Ethos focuses on the concept that if you are good than the world is also good for you. So, every individual should an effective management and balance of personal and work life in the organization.
4. The divine element, which is a inner part of an individual, is a part of cosmic or pure consciousness. It gives a base for mutual trust, cooperative, teamwork and common good.

5. The Indian Ethos gives much importance not to the knowledge but to character. It is the character, which is the real power and wealth.
6. Indian Ethos are based on Indian scripture like – Shruties of Gita and Upanishad and Smruties of Puranas. Indian thought provides the whole – man approach through knowledge of creation, cosmos and internal relation between spiritual and materialistic life.
7. Indian Ethos works with a fact that all work is worthfull and honourable. 'Work is worship' is the guiding principle for all effort as advocated in the Indian ethos.
8. Indian Ethos rarely talks of rights and prevails ages. It always emphasizes only on duty and responsibility of human being.
9. Indian Ethos deals with two types of knowledge (a) knowledge of creation (b) knowledge of creator. It means the objective as well as the subjective knowledge, which mix a balance of cosmic life.

The Bhagavad Gita analyse (and discuss with a sharp insight the concepts which we are using for modern management like vision, leadership, motivation, excellence in work, achieving goals, attitude towards work, nature of individual decision-making planning etc.

Lord Krishna raised the levels of Arjuna's mind with his inspiring words to come in the state of right action, faith in himself and self-confidence in the ultimate victory of 'Dharma.' These, guidelines direct and protect us in performing our tasks in business world and global environment also. These are the basic principles of human life. By following these anyone can achieve his goals successfully in any field of life. The main motive is to make develop smart, responsible and work committed personality, which can serve the society and make a harmonious environment.

Work: In whole universe, when we see all around, some actions or activities are going on. Every creature of this universe is indulged in something. This is a type of work. Like all other creatures, man is also always involved in some action or activity. It is said that, "Man is a congenital worker." Except the sleeping hours, every moment some activities are going on. And the activities or action performed for a result or purpose is 'work'.

In our family or society every responsible person is a worker. Either it is a peon or a manager of organization; he is performing his duty or task. He is working. In his working, he is also learning or being trained and then he gets promotion. Even the owner and entrepreneur are also engaged in some duties. It is work, these are different purpose for different individual to work. We can summaries some purposes here:

To earn livelihood

To discharge family and social duties

To actualize their talents and capabilities

To leave some enduring creation behind him

To earn reputation and recognition

"Work is the application of discretion within limits in order to produce a result."

By Albert Law

Work and Activities

Work is a result oriented and discretionary action, while activity is neither.

Work requires discretion and discretion means the total human being in action.

The most super-ordinate character of work ethic is 'sacrifice'.

It can be expressed as 'serving society or world'.

Now it is expressed as **work-commitment**

This is for society through the family, the organization, the nation and so on.

From management point of view:-

This work commitment or sacrifice is in the form of 'total man in the use and style of discretion.

The same determination is needed to better leadership and more effective teamwork.

It is responsibility-orientation

Work Ethos

Ethos refers to the activities or action what we perform and what one ought to perform. In modern management arena we will discuss the work ethos of management people or leaders of modern society.

We can measure the ethos at four levels or four pillars:

1. **Striving for excellence** – Every worker or professional try to perform in the best way he can. This is called striving for excellence. This excellence requires mastery of theoretical knowledge as well as practical skills of the job. Then an enthusiasm for applying solution to a problem has importance.
2. **Motivation of Service** – When a person or a professional is performing his job, a motivational factor is affecting or accelerating his work. If there is no motivation, we can't expect success of work and this motivation is very important for services or to serve the society.
3. **Abiding sense of responsibility** – A professional ought to be very conscience of his prime responsibility to use his wisdom, knowledge, skills as well as power and authority for helping the people and social betterment. A person is morally responsible to several groups and different job and he has to perform the entire task in proper way.
4. **Professional Integrity** – It is expected that professional will perform their duties correctly, impartially and without fear or favour. He should not mislead any person and also not favour in out of way. They should also not make false claim about their qualification, specialization or experience.

There are the work ethos by which we can make a good culture and commitment to work for better productivity of the organization for the welfare of the society and development of people of the organization.

The Bhagavad Gita analysis and discuss with a sharp insight. the concepts which we are using for modern management like vision, leadership, motivation, excellence in work, achieving goals, attitude towards work, nature of individual decision making planning etc.

Sri Krishna raised the levels of Arjuna's mind with his inspiring words to come in the state of right action, faith in himself and self confidence in the ultimate victory of 'Dharma.' These guidelines direct and protect us in performing our tasks in business world and global environment also. These are the basic principles of human life. By following these any one can achieve his goals successfully in any field of life. The main motive is to make and develop and smart, responsible and work committed personality which can serve the society and make a harmonious environment.

30

Vedanta and Managers

Modern management are increasingly adopting Vedic percepts to overcome the competition and stay in the race of marketshare.

The Vedas are a systematic and formulated study of the science of life.

Various MNC's have started adopting the teachings given by Vedas and Upnishads.

The word 'Veda' originates from the Sanskrit root 'Vid, which means 'to know'.

The managers get an indept knowledge and insight to the **understanding of how the work should be done, what are the work ethics** etc. by going through the Vedas.

The ancient scriptures provides the managers lessons of:

1. **Nishkam Karma** is work must be done without personal claims which means desireless work should be the main way of doing work.
2. Work is worship
3. Propkar punyay, papaya parpidnam i.e. it is virtue to help other and sin to harass other.
4. **Yoga Karmasu Kaushalam** i.e. excellence of work through self motivation and self development.

5. "**Vasudhaiva Kutunbkam**" : Treat everyone as friends and the entire world as one family.

However the various lessons that a manager can learn from the Vedas are as follows:

1. **Foster Team Spirit:** The manager should learn to have a control on such attributes as ego, self-centrism etc. in order to enhance the competitive spirit and to effectively delegate work. The managers should learn to work and foster team spirit.
2. **Take Responsibility :** The Vedas also enlighten the managers with respect to quality of **taking responsibility.**

   The teachings from Vedas also make people learn the importance of not fearing from failure but to try and try until you succeed.

   The Vedas also teach not to run awry from your responsibilities or apportion blame.
3. **Share the Credit :** The scriptures also emphasise on the fact that it is the moral responsibility of the managers to share the credit with his team, peers, colleagues etc.

   The credit be it financial, recognition or praise etc. should be shared with the desiring workers.
4. **Welcome Competition:** Dvaita i.e. Duality is the law of Nature. Happiness-Sorrow; Success-Failure; Pleasure-Pain all are an inseparable part of life. The competition should also be taken as a positive energy or motivation to work. The teachings from Indian scriptures preached of accepting a healthy competition so as to enhance their capabilities.
5. **Praise Counts:** The Vedas also encourages the manager's ability to motivate his colleagues and subordinates.

   Certain management philosophers are of the belief that motivation through money is not the only tool for encouraging employees but certain non-monetary motivations like appreciation and giving recognition are also important.
6. **Stay Focussed:** The managers while making decisions may get involved in storm of opposition regarding the rational method of achieving goals.

   The Vedas and ancient literature preaches that in such a situation the managers must **stay calm, focused** and **practice meditation.**

7. **Character Building:** The lessons from Ancient Indian Scriptures laid emphasis on the Character Building of any individual.

   Character is the most powerful guarantor of a personality which makes an individual perfect.

8. **Spirit of Cooperation:** Through various teachings of Vedas the spirit of cooperation has also been emphasised.

9. **Emphasis on Loyalty and Gratitude:** Loyalty and Gratitude to the organization and colleagues should become important peatures of professionalism.

10. **Work Commitment:** Advices from holy scriptures say non-attachment to the fruits or results of actions performed in the course of one's duty. The teachings emphazise upon **work-commitment**.

11. **Utilization of Available Resources:** The mangers also learn to use available resources optimally, reduction in wastages so as to cut down the operation cost and thereby maximize profits.

12. **Removal of Self-Ego:** Ego is the main enemy of humanity which separates one person from other. This ego stops the development of both mental and physical abilities. The thought that:

    "I am the super, I can do everything"- stops the learning and observing skill of an individual.

13. **Value Based Decision-Making:** The teachings preach that decisions should be based on basic values of spirituality, ethics and ecological positivity and negativity.

14. **Forming a Vision and Planning the strategy to realize such Vision** is another lesson to be learned from the teachings.

15. To establish the Institutional Excellence and to build an Innovative Organization is also to be learned.

16. **Integrity Counts:** Another lesson to be learned by a manager is that the means to the goals must be as upright as the goal. It is important to pay as much attention to the means of work as to its ends.

    The managers should understand that success through wrong means cab be achieved but it minuses the peace of mind.

17. **Remember your Teams is Human:** The Vedas also preach that do not expect every employee to be consistent with the pace that the mangers or on individual sets.

It is essential to give break to the teammembers and give some time as well to complete their tasks. Thus, making them relaxed and wanted.

Thus, the teachings from Vedas try to develop and promote a Culture of Octapace i.e., Openness, Co-operation, Trust, Authority, Participation, Autonomy, Collaboration and Empathy, wherein the managers can develop Creativity, Innovation, Maximum Profits, **Partnership**, **Excellence in Work**, commitment etc.

All the modern management concepts like Vision, Leadership, Motivation, Excellence in Work, Planning, Achievement of Goals, Meaning of Work, Decision Making, Nature of Individual etc. all are derived from the Vedanta.

31

Indian Heritage in Production and Consumption

Our Dependence on the Environment

We are living in the age of modern science and technology, and in this age, most of the people are moving towards the urban society. Although our urban way of life seems to separate us from nature, we are intimately connected to, and dependent on, natural processes.

First, all our production depends on the availability of resources. Some of these resources are renewable, such as wood from our forests, water from lakes and rivers and the oxygen in the air we breathe. Renewable resources are regenerated by natural processes, and can be used indefinitely provided that our rate of extraction does not exceed their regeneration rates.

Other resources are nonrenewable, meaning that there is no regeneration process, at least not within a length of time that has any meaning for us. Such resources include fossil fuels (coal, petroleum, natural gas) and metals. Consumption of these resources inevitably reduces their availability in the future.

Second, we depend on our environment as a dump for our waste products. We put solid wastes into landfills, release effluents into our streams, and exhaust waste gases into the atmosphere.

Although our developed technology has introduced many new ways of utilizing resources and creating waste products, these two general processes are fundamental to all production and, indeed, to the most basic processes of life. This leads us to recognize a third way in which we are tied to our environment - we rely on the natural services it provides.

One crucial environmental service has already been mentioned: the regeneration of renewable resources. Trees grow from seed, producing more wood. The water cycle, by processes of evaporation, precipitation and filtration, reproduces clean water. Photosynthesizing plant life produces oxygen.

Such processes provide a second type of service as well - the absorption and conversion of wastes. For example, waste material on a forest floor is decomposed by numerous types of organisms (worms, microbes, etc.), fertilizing the soil and feeding the growth of new plant life. Waste water is cleaned by aquatic organisms that play similar roles of decomposition and filtration. And the process of photosynthesis that produces oxygen also removes carbon dioxide, the waste product we exhale.

A third set of services are the natural regulatory functions. Examples include: the balance of gases in the atmosphere (including everything from oxygen content to upper-atmosphere ozone that filters out UV radiation), temperature regulation (how much solar energy is absorbed in comparison to what is radiated into space), water runoff and erosion control, formation of fertile topsoil, and the balancing of the chemical composition of the oceans.

Production and Consumption

If we look at such systems on the largest scale, that of the Earth as a whole, we can see that there are two fundamental flows: a flow of energy, and a flow of materials. The flow of energy is linear. That is, the energy moves in a line from source to sink, powering production between the two. The sun provides the steady source of radioactive energy that powers natural production. This energy is used and inevitably degraded into waste heat that is radiated into space (the energy sink).

The natural flow of materials is circular rather than linear: Materials are used repeatedly, round and round the food chains. The primary producers - photosynthesizing plants - build organic materials from soil minerals and carbon dioxide, driven by solar energy. Animals (including humans) then consume these plant materials for energy and for materials to use in growth, or consume other animals for the same purposes. Dead plants and animals are used as food by the decomposers (worms, moulds, microbes, etc.) and their waste products are in turn used as material input for plant growth, completing the cycle. In short, waste products at each stage are utilized by some other organism as food, with the entire process driven by energy from the sun.

Even our use of fossil fuels for energy and for materials production (e.g. plastics) is dependent on these natural cycles. Here too we are consuming materials that were organically produced utilizing, and storing, energy from the sun. The difference is that this production occurred many millions of years before our time. These materials are the buried legacy of ancient natural cycles. On our time scale, they are nonrenewable, and will eventually be depleted to levels that will make their extraction too expensive to be economic.

Our Way of Doing Business

In contrast to these natural cycles, which are sustainable, our way of running our economy cannot be sustained.

Rather than relying on the constant flow of energy available from the sun, we are consuming ancient stored energy (fossil fuels) that cannot be restored short of geological time scales.

Furthermore, our materials processing is linear rather than cyclical. That is, we extract resources, steadily depleting them (whether or not they are in principle renewable). We then use them to produce what we want for consumption. Most waste products from our use of these goods are then simply dumped: gases into the air, liquids into our streams, and solids into landfills. Thus we have the twin problems of resource depletion and pollution.

A sustainable economy must be cyclical in its processing of materials. As much as possible, waste products from one industry need to serve as resources for other industries. That is, our economy needs to mimic sustainable natural processes, where one organism's waste is another's food.

Another way of characterizing this situation makes use of the concept of natural capital. Capital is a stock (collection, aggregate) of something that produces a flow (a periodic yield) of valuable goods or services. A stock of factory machinery (manufactured capital) produces a flow of automobiles. Financial capital (such as a bond) provides a flow of monetary payments. This same concept applies to natural stocks as well. Natural capital in the form of a forest produces a flow of goods in the form of new trees. It also provides a flow of services in the form of oxygen, erosion control, wildlife habitats, etc. The flows are income. Depleting the stocks is capital consumption. Just as it is financially ruinous for a company to consume its capital (manufactured or financial), it is ruinous for our society to destroy natural capital.

This unsustainable structure of our economy is creating increasing environmental problems as its scale increases. That is, the growth of such an economy aggravates its problems. The feature that determines economic scale in a linear economy is **throughput:** the volume of materials flowing from the environment (resource use), through the economy (human production, exchange, and consumption), and back to the environment as wastes. Throughput in turn is determined by two factors: the number of people participating in the economy (total human population), and the per-capita resource use by each of these individuals. The biggest growth in each of these factors is currently split between different parts of the world. In general, developing (poor) countries are contributing the most to population growth, while the developed (rich) countries continue to increase their per-capita usage of resources.

Our fundamental environmental problem is growth of throughput. Waste disposal becomes pollution when natural systems cannot absorb and recycle our waste products, resulting in smog, fouled water or poisoned land. Resources are depleted when natural regeneration cannot keep up with our increasing rates of extraction, as in the cases of east coast codfish or west coast salmon. The increasing scale of our economy eliminates habitat and causes the extinction of increasing numbers of species, many of which likely had roles in the environmental services we need.

These problems with the way we do business can also be characterized in ethical terms. They reflect the kind of problem we have seen in other contexts where self-interest is not adequately balanced against the interests of others. Specifically, our environmental problems are, for the most part, **free-rider** problems. Virtually all of us have been, in one way or another, getting free rides at the expense of others.

Simply put, the environmental costs of our production and consumption have not been factored into the prices of the goods and services we consume. Environmental costs are externalities. For example, petroleum is priced as a commodity: Its price is determined simply by how much supply is currently coming out of the ground in relation to current demand. But the depletion of this resource, its decreased availability for future use, is not coasted. On the contrary, we compensate oil companies for the depletion of this resource. So petroleum extractors take a free ride in a double sense - not only do they avoid paying the cost of depletion (to be eventually paid by future generations), but they are provided with financial incentives to do so more rapidly!

Petroleum, as it is used, creates waste products: burned gasoline is the major contributor to smog problems, and various plastics and toxic chemicals (products of the petrochemical industry) must eventually be disposed of. As with petroleum producers, petroleum consumers get free rides. Each of us, in driving our vehicles or in using chemicals, contributes to pollution problems. But the costs of such pollution are not factored into the prices of the products we buy. Health problems due to smog are not incorporated into the price of gasoline, but are instead covered by our health system out of general tax revenues. Likewise, the price of toxic chemicals does not include the costs of cleaning up toxic waste dumps. Again, such costs are being increasingly carried by the taxpayer.

In a free market system, consumers choose the products they use based on price and quality comparisons. If all costs, including environmental costs, were included in the price of a product (such as gasoline), then more environmentally benign alternatives could compete more effectively.

The free rides we take at the expense of future generations are not confined to the depletion of nonrenewable resources, or the creation of pollution problems. Damage to environmental services is also ignored in our pricing mechanisms. For example, timber extracted from a forest is typically priced simply as a commodity (how current supply extracted compares to current demand). No costs are attached to the loss of forest as habitat, protector of watersheds, maintainer of microclimate, or biodiversity storehouse.

The same point can be repeated in terms of capital and income: Manufactured capital is depreciated in recognition that its value declines each year as it wears out or is used up, but the use or loss of natural capital is not counted as a charge against current income. A sustainable system is one with sustainable income - one which preserves its natural capital to ensure the future flow of that income.

When the scale of human activity was small in comparison to the whole world, we could get away with taking these free rides. Although humans exploited other species to extinction even in prehistoric times, and have repeatedly turned fertile agricultural lands into arid wastelands, such disasters were always localized, and other natural resources were always available for exploitation. But as the size of our economy grows, such impacts can no longer be ignored. We now operate on a global scale, and there is nowhere else to go.

Present ways of doing business are simply not sustainable. That is, our ways of doing business cannot be maintained into future generations (our children and grandchildren). We cannot continue economic growth - the growth in throughput that exhausts resources and overwhelms waste disposal and environmental services.

A sustainable economy requires:

1. For renewable resources (fish, forests, etc.), the rate of harvest should not exceed the rate of regeneration.
2. The rate at which we allow economic activity to generate wastes that must be passed into the environment should not be allowed to exceed the environment's ability to absorb them.
3. The depletion of nonrenewable resources (oil, coal, etc.) should be offset by investment in and development of renewable substitutes for them.

We can say that our whole production and consumption process is dependent and directed by natural resources.

32

Personal Growth and Lessons from Ancient Educational System

The ancient Indian Educational System was based on the philosophy that deals with life and existence of self and realization of self and attainment of fearless bliss or pure consciousness.

The Ancient Indian Educational System can be summarized in the following model:

Education → Values → Principles → Wisdom

- The main purpose of Ancient Indian Educational System was to know our culture, our social values and to make ideal human or civilian.
- According to the culture and values, the principles governing the code of conduct were made.
- This resulted in the attainment of Wisdom by adopting and implementing the principles.
- Through this process, the motto of building responsible person was achieved.

Features of Ancient Indian Educational System

The features of Ancient Indian Educational System in Vedic age were:

1. **Gurukul:** Gurukul was the home of Gurus or Acharyas which were free from government control and influence or interference. The students used to stay away from their home for concentration and devotion to their work and knowledge.
2. **Ideals of Vedic Gurus/Teachers:** The ideals of Gurus were of the highest caliber both from knowledge and spiritual viewpoint. They possessed great influence and high reputation and paid full attention towards development of qualities of their students.
3. **Duties of Shishyas:** The duty of the shishyas (disciples) was to obey and serve his/her Guru.
4. **Guru-Shishya Relation:** Guru and Shishya relation was like that of father and son.
5. **Child Education:** The education in ancient times used to begin from the start of childhood.
6. **Multiple Course of Study:** The Vedic students took the education of Vedas, Sutras and Upanishads, Vyakran, Jyothish etc.
7. **Equal Opportunity to Gain Education:** During this period, everyone was eligible to gain higher education irrespective of caste, colour, religion or creed.
8. **Attention to Women Education:** Women education too received proper attention in the Vedic Age, and was called as Rishikas.
9. **Physical Education:** The Students also used to gain education of various Arts and Grafts as Agriculture, Animal Husbandry etc.

Teaching from Ancient Indian Educational System

For the attainment of personal growth and for building responsible human begins, various Indian Scriptures have contributed. The personal growth depends upon the lessons to be learned from ancient texts such as:

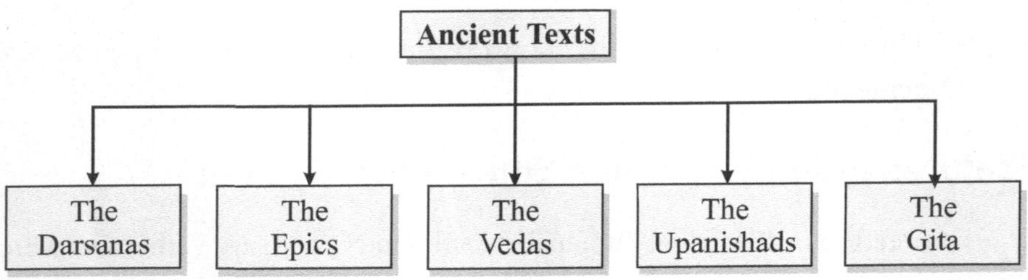

Various Indian texts such as The Upanishads, The Vedas, The Major Epics as Ramayana and Mahabharata, The Panchtantra stories and The Jataka Tales give lessons to human relations, of propriety and of justice which are concerns of a common man, King or as of Today's managers.

I. The Darsanas

Concepts which are basic in Indian tradition are contained in the ancient texts like the Vedas and the Upanishads. Collectively these are called the 'Darsanas'.

The word "Darsana", derived from 'Darsan' (to see) used as they contain the quintessence of what the sages of yore had seen or experienced, **through observation and analysis**.

The Darsanas are believed to be the creations of not one mind, each one the six systems of philosophy contained is associated with the name of principal interpreter.

The teachings from Darsanas provide that all lead to the same end, **knowledge of one Supreme Conciousness.**

The teachings of Darsanas are not abstract truth, but have the validity of verified truth. Physical phenomenon are verified in the laboratory and can be seen and confirmed by others, however, verification of non-physical phenomenon has to depend on observation, comparisons and intellectual analysis.

Based on this, when they saw that the growth of plant was dependent on the sunlight, they conceptualized the sun as a source of all energy. The result was **Gayatri Mantra**.

When they observed that one was primary and the other members were deriving there from, they said that the Ultimate Reality was one, without which there cannot be another. This one was named as Brahman.

However, Darsanas provide lessons for philosophy or attitude of life and living. They contain principles to guide one's life.

II. The Epics

Epics are stories told to communicate the lessons of Darsanas, such as The Mahabharata, The Ramayana, The Panchtantra and The Jataka Tales.

These Epics used characters from the real world. The events in the epics are believed to have actually happened and the characters acquire dimensions of perfection of Virtue or viciousness. They are the models to follow or to avoid.

Many researchers draw lessons in Management from the Epics. This is so, as the stories are about the Kings and the relationships. Managers of business organizations and officers of the government can benefit from the behaviours of the characters in the epics.

III. The Vedas

The word 'Veda' originates from the Sanskrit root 'Vid' which means '**to know**'. The word Veda means knowledge. When it is applied to scripture, it signifies a book of knowledge. The Vedas are the foundational scriptures of the Hindus.

The Vedas are in 4 parts:

1. The Rig Veda
2, The Sama Veda
3 The Yajur Veda
4 The Artha Veda

They are also called as the Sruthis. These Vedas can be further divided into two parts:

i The Karma Kanda- devoted to work
ii. The Jnana Kanda- devote to knowledge

The teachings enshrined in these Vedas give an idea as to how the work should be done, what are work ethics etc., and also emphasizes on the knowledge and learning attitude which should be followed by the people.

IV. The Upanishads

The Upanishads provide the latter part of the Vedas, (also called Vedanta, meaning the end of Vedas), comprise of sections dealing with knowledge.

The teachings in Upanishads provide detail ways of attaining the 4 goals viz., Dharma, Artha, Kama and Moksha. These contain the essence of Vedantic Ethics Artha (wealth) and Kama (desire) are integrated with Dharma and Moksha. They preach that both wealth and desires are recognized as legitimate goals, provided they are within the limits of Dharma and Moksha.

The Upanishads provides for lessons such as:-

1. Nishkam Karma i.e., work must be done without personal claims, which means desireless work should be the main way of doing work.
2. Work is Worship.
3. Propkar punyay, papaya parpidnam i.e., it is virtue to help others and sin to harass others.
4. Yogh Karmasu Kaushalam i.e., Excellence of Work through self motivation and self development.
5. 'Vasudhaiva Kutumbkam': Treat everyone as friends and the entire world as one family.

However, the Upanishads do not demand that one should live a life of poverty and total renunciation of all comforts.

V. The Gita

The Bhagawad Gita is the most precious part of the Mahabharata and is acknowledged as one of the supreme treasures of ancient human literature. It involves teachings of human existence and of the Vedic lessons. The Gita is the teachings (exhortations) of the Lord Krishna to Lord Arjuna.

The exhortation of the Lord Krishna focuses on :

- One has to do his duty. We have no rights on the fruits of the work. While doing one's duty, do not think of the rewards of self.
- Realization is the highest state of human consciousness.
- The feeling of I and mine should be given up and see everything equal.
- Detachment to perishable things and attachment to only God will give peace of mind.
- God is within us.
- God is the only reality, truth and live for God alone.
- Avoid self-praise.
- Supreme knowledge is ultimate devotion to God.
- Make God your friend, philosopher and guide.
- Be sincere in all works, Work is Worship.

Management Guidelines from The Bhagawad Gita:

There is an important distinction between effectiveness and efficiency in managing:

Effectiveness is doing the right things and efficiency is doing things right.

The general principles of effective management can be applied in every fields the differences being mainly in the application than in principles. Again, effective management is not limited in its application only to business or industrial enterprises but to all organisations where the aim is to reach a given goal through a Chief Executive or a Manager with the help of a group of workers.

The **Manager's functions** can be briefly summed up as under:

- Forming a vision and planning the strategy to realize such vision.
- Cultivating the art of leadership.
- Establishing the institutional excellence and building an innovative organization.
- Developing human resources.
- Teambuilding and teamwork.
- Delegation, motivation, and communication and
- Reviewing performance and taking corrective steps whenever called for.

Thus Management is a process in search of excellence to align people and get them committed to work for a common goal to the maximum social benefit.

The various teachings of Hindu Scriptures have identified the following Mantras which help to face various challenges and for making rational decisions which are as follows:

1. **Choose your vocation wisely:** Follow your Swadharm, i.e., your inherent nature. Choose a field of activity that fire your passion and is compatible with your nature to achieve a higher degree of recognition and success, which will also help to get money as per your liking.
2. **Foster Team Spirit:** The teachings impart the lessons to have control on such attributes like ego, self-centrism etc. in order to enhance the competition and to effectively delegate work. The ancient teachings emphasize on understanding the importance of collectivity and teamwork.

3. **Praise Counts:** The Vedas also encourages the manager's ability to motivate his colleagues and subordinates. Certain management philosophers are of the belief that motivation through money is not the only tool for encouraging employees but certain non-monetary motivators like appreciation and giving recognition are also important.
4. **Take Responsibility:** The Vedas also enlighten the managers with respect to quality of **taking responsibility.** The teachings from the Vedas also make people learn the importance of not fearing from failure but to try and try until you succeed. It also make people understand that never run away from your responsibility or apportion blame.
5. **Share the Credit:** The ancient scriptures also emphasized on the fact that is the moral responsibility of the manager to share the credit with his ream, peers, colleagues, etc. The credit be it financial, recognition or praise etc. should be shared with the deserving workers.
6. **Welcome Competition:** Dvaita i.e., Duality is the law of the nature. Happiness-Sorrow; Success-Failure; Pleasure-Pain all are an inseparable part of life. The competition should also be taken as a positive energy or motivation to work. The teachings from Indian Scriptures preached of accepting a healthy competition so as to enhance their capabilities.
7. **Peace of Mind:** The means to achieve the goal must be as upright as the goal. According to Swami Vivekananda, "one of the greatest lessons I have learnt in my life is to pay as much attention to the means of work as to its ends." Thus, success achieved through wrong means comes but it minuses the peace of mind.
8. **Tay Focused:** The managers while making decisions may get involved in storm of opposition regarding the rational method of achieving goals. The Vedas and the ancient literature preach that in such a situation the managers must **stay calm, focused** and **practice meditation**. These 3 ways would help the managers to have a higher level of consciousness and top the enormous power of **Inner Self.**
9. **Character Building:** The lessons from Ancient Indian Educational System laid emphasis on the character building of any individual. Character is the most powerful guarantor of a personality which makes an individual perfect.
10. **Personal Growth:** The motto of Ancient Indian Educational System was based on the personal development of an individual. It laid emphasis

on the knowledge of different physical and spiritual skills and intelligence to do the work effectively.

11. **Removal of Self-Ego:** Ego is the main enemy of humanity which separates one person from other. This ego stops the development of both mental and physical abilities. The thought that:- "I can the Super, I can do everything"- stops the learning and observing skill of an individual.
12. **Spirit of Cooperation:** Through various teachings the spirit of cooperation has also been emphasized.
13. **Value-based decision making:** The teachings preach that decisions should be based on basic values of spirituality, ethics and ecological positivism and negativism.
14. **Emphasis on Loyalty and Gratitude:** Loyalty and Gratitude to the organization and colleagues should become important features of professionalism.
15. **Forming a Vision and Planning the strategy to realize such a Vision:** is another lesson to be learned from the teachings.
16. **To cultivate the Art of Leadership:** is also another lesson to be learned.
17. **To establish the Institutional Excellence and to build an Innovative Organization:** is also to be learned.
18. **To review the performance and to take corrective steps whenever called for:** is also another value being emphasized by the ancient scriptures.
19. **Work Commitment:** Advices from Holy Scriptures say non-attachment to the fruits or results of actions performed in the course of one's duty. If we are calculating date of promotion for putting in our efforts, then such work cannot be commitment-oriented causing excellence in the results but it will be promotion-oriented resulting in inevitable disappointments.
20. **Attitude Towards Work:** The Gita tells us to develop the visionary perspective of the work we do, i.e., to develop a sense of larger vision in one's work for common good.
21. **Utilization of Available resources:** The lessons from the Holy Gita preach us to choose wisely and utilize optimally the scarce resources if one has to succeed in his venture.

22. **Evolving Daivi Work Culture:** In Gita Shri Krishna elaborates on 2 types of Work Ethics i.e.,

    (a) **Daivi Work Culture** or Divine Work Culture: means fearlessness, purify, gentleness, self-control, sacrifice, straight-forwardness, absence of fault finding and greed, envy and pride.

    (b) **Asuri Work Culture** or Demonic Work Culture: means egoism, delusion, desire-centric, improper performance, work which is not oriented towards service.

The teachings emphasizes on the creation of Daivi work culture.

Thus, it is clear that ancient educational system gives a broad spectrum of personal and professional life where we can grow ourselves in the field of working. All the modem management concepts like Vision, Leadership, Motivation, Excellence in Work, Achievement of Goals, Meaning of Work, Attitude towards Work, Nature of an individual, Decision-Making, Planning etc., are all derived from various Ancient Indian Scriptures.

33

Total Quality Management : An Indian Insight

Total Quality Management (TQM) is a philosophy that involves everyone is an organization in a continual effort to **improve quality** and **achieve customer satisfaction**.

It is an approach to business. It looks critically not only at products and services which a company provides in relation to the processes but it also employs to create them.

Total Quality is "fully satisfying agreed customer requirements at the lowest interval cost".

This means focusing our concentration on doing things right the first time rather than making and then co-uting errors or defects.

The term TQM comprises of 3 perspectives :

(i) Total

(ii) Quality

(iii) Management

Total

Total encompasses everything the company does, all its process and employees at every level I the company at all times.

It is an overall organizational strategy which is formulated at the top level management and speared throughout the entire organization.

It also involves the **internal customers** (those who receive the work of another within the company) and **external customers** (who create a chain of quality, which eventually reaches the customer).

Quality

Quality is a relative term, generally used with reference to the end use of a product or service.

Quality is "**fitness for use**"

Quality is "**Conformance to requirements**"

Quality of a product or service is its ability to satisfy the needs and expectations of the customers.

Management

TQM is a managerial approach. It is headed and coordinated by the TQM Project Manager.

He should be able to understand the process and train other people in TQM and reports directly to the GM or CEO.

As all people, from the bottom to top are involved in this function, it is a **People-Oriented and Mgmt. Approach**.

Thus, TQM is a management philosophy embracing all activities through which the needs and expectations of the customers and the community and the objective of the organization are satisfied in the most efficient and effective way by maximizing the potential of employees in a continuous drive for improvement.

Underlying Principles

The underlying principles behind TQM efforts are:

- Customer satisfaction
- Continuous improvement
- Management-by-fact
- All functions are interdependent
- Participative and integrated Problem Solving Process
- Every workstation a control point

Features

TQM plays a major role in bringing a change.

The following are the basic features of TQM:

1. TQM is a **pragmatic long-term** systems approach:

   TQM is a concept which can be adopted and practiced through proper planning, systematic evaluation and allocating responsibilities and resources. It is not a one-time strategy but a long-term continuous approach.

2. TQM is **initiated** and driven by **top management**

   TQM is a strategic direction and can be trigger by the top management. Developing organizational vision mission, philosophy, strategies, objectives and plans is the responsibility of the Top Mgmt. Therefore, Top Mgmt. needs to be involved in TQM and the Quality Improvement Process, and should be thinking of ways to bring about Innovations.

2. TQM aims at bringing about a **Total Cultural Change** in every facet of the organization.

   TQM creates an organizational culture which is conducive to continuous improvements.

4. TQM **interlinks** and **integrates** the various subsystems of the organisation:

   Each department in the organization strives for excellence and tries to achieve its set objectives. The TQM tries to break down the barriers between the departments and integrates the objectives of various departments with the main objective of the organization as to follow the same common unified approach of meeting the customers requirements.

5. TQM requires involvement, participation and cross-functional management

   The objectives of TQM can not be achieved unless there is participation of all, at different levels in the problem solving process. By forming cross-functional quality improvement terms, TQM overcomes this barrier.

6. TQM aims at meeting the dynamic needs of the customer and creates loyal and diversified customer base.

   The TQM recognizes customers both as internal and external. It tries to create a diversified and loyal customer base which promotes the profitability of the organization and helps to withstand any competition.

POTENTIAL BENEFITS OF TQM

The advantages of adopting TQM system are:

1. TQM helps to **focus** clearly on the **needs of the market.**

   TQM focuses on the concept of universality it trice to abstract the satisfaction perceptions of market and thus helps the organization to identify and meet the requirements of the market in a better way.

2. TQM **facilitates** to aspire for a **top quality performer** in every sphere of activity.

   The negative attitudes of employees and the non-participative culture of the organization pose the greatest hurdle to organisation's **success**, **growth** and **prosperity**. TQM emphasizes on bringing about the attitudinal and cultural change through the **promotion of participative work culture** and **effective term-work**.

   This helps to achieve **recognition** and **self-development** and **enhances employee's interest** in the job.

3. It **channelises** the procedures necessary to achieve **quality performance**.

   To achieve quality a **systematic** and a **long-term planning** and **strategic approach**. By focusing on defining the quality policies, goals and objectives and communicating these properly to one and all in the organization, by adopting various techniques and developing and using a system of evaluation, the organizaions can channelize their efforts to achieve the desired and objectivated quality performance.

4. It helps examine **critically and continuously** all processes to remove non-productive activities and waste.

   The organizations always aim at improving productivity as it leads to reduction in cost resulting in increase in profitability. Due to the formation of **Quality Improvement Teams** which meet regularly and through a systematic approach which tries to remove non-productive activity. A continuous effort to identify the problems and resolve them helps to reduce the waste. The TQM culture thus improves **housekeeping, cost-effectiveness** and **safety.**

5. It **gears** organizations to fully understand the **competition** and **develop** an effective combating strategy.

It is essential for the organizations to understand the competition and develop and adopt suitable strategies to meet the challenge. TQM helps to understand the pulse of the customers and thus the market, it gives an edge to the organization to meet the competition.

6. It **helps** to develop **good procedures** for the **communication** and **acknowledging good work**.

   Improper procedures and inadequate communication may result in misunderstanding, confusion, low productivity, duplication of efforts, poor quality, low moral etc. TQM **binds** together the members of various related sections, departments and different levels of management thereby providing an effective vehicle of communication and interaction.

7. It help to review the process needed to develop the strategy of never ending improvement. TQM emphasizes on a continuous and periodic review in order to make the required changes.

   Thus, there are various benefits derived by the organization with regard to TQM. Many of these benefits include **enrichment of work life** which are not quantifiable.

   The various tangible and intangible benefits of TQM are :

Benefits of TQM

Tangible Gains	Intangible Gains
– Better Product Quality	– Effective Teamwork
– Productivity Improvement	– Enhancement of Job Interest
– Reduced Quality Cost	– Improvement in human relations and work area moral
– Increased Market	– Customer satisfaction
– Reduced Employee Grievances	– Improved Communication
	– Enhanced problem-solving capacity
	– Improved corporate health and character of the company
	– Better Company Image

Part - VII

Stress Management

34

Stress Management

Stress is a physiological and psychological imbalance. It arises due to the demands on a person and that person's inability to meet these demands. It means when the demand of a person is more and his output is less because of failure, he suffers from anxiety and dissatisfaction. Normally, when we have a lot of work to do and we are not able to complete the work, we experience a sense of anxiety, unfulfillment, dissatisfaction, worry and finally an unpleasant feeling. It affects our psychological and mental state and ultimately the capacity to perform.

Definitions:

Different disciplines and different professionals have viewed it differently. In physics, stress is a force which acts on a body to produce strain. In physiology, the various changes in the physiological functions in response to evocative agents denote stress (rather that strain). In psychology, stress refers to a particular kind of state of the organization resulting from some interaction between him/her and the environment.

One of the most commonly accepted view of stress is provided by Hens Selye (1956). He called it "General Adaptation Syndrome (GAS)" which has been widely held as a comprehensive model to explain the stress phenomenon.

Selye defines stress as "an adoptive response to the external situation that results in physical, psychological, and/or behavioural deviation for organizational participants"

He has suggested a THREE-STAGE MODEL and states that when an organism is confronted with a threat, the general physiological response occurs in three stages:

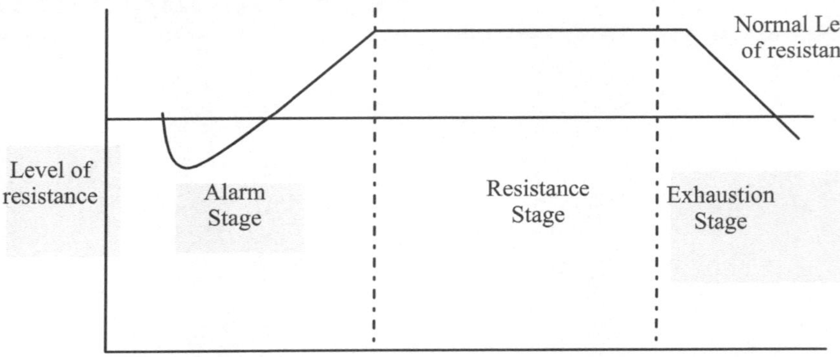

Duration of exposure of stress
"General Adaptation Syndrome"

1. **Alarm Stage: -** In this stage, the body's response to or familiarizing itself with the new situation or stressor* (A stressor is a factor or stimulant that creates stress). At this stage, an individual is under Eustress.
2. **Resistance stage:** Which involves resisting and reaching to the situation? In this stage, an individual is in a flight or fight situation. In this situation, the body prepares to either escape from the situation or to survive in it.
3. **Exhaustion Stage:** It is the next stage of resistance? If the resistance stage goes on for a long period, then the person becomes distressed.

Another commonly accepted view of stress is given by Panels. He called it "Burn Out Stress Syndrome (BOSS)".

He has suggested a five-stage model for defining the stress.

(i) **Honey moon Stage:-** At this stage, person performs the function at introduction level. He is very enthusiastic about his work. In spite of workload he does not feel any kind of frustration or illness. This is the initial stage of Stress.

(ii) **Fuel shortage Stage:-** under this stage a person feels fatigue, confusion and looses his confidence because of stress. But his adoption energy assists him to adjust according to the circumstances for a limited period of time.

(iii) **Chronic Stage:-** At this stage, person tries to escape from the situation.

(iv) **Crisis Stage:-** It is slightly more harmful than chronic stage. Person feels a lot of mental stress in this stage.

(v) **Hitting the wall Stage:-** It is completely exhausted stage. Under it, the person lost his confidence completely. Adaptation energy ends and the body do not give any kind of support.

Affect of stress according to this model

1. Depletion of energy resources.
2. Reduced resistance levels
3. Absenteeism and inefficiency at work
4. Pessimism and dissatisfaction

Persons experiencing stress but having frustration, tolerance capacity may be able to manage it temporarily. But those who do not have stress tolerance capacity, would get excessively upset and angry unreasonably when it further crosses the limit. They will be physically ill in addition to mental illness.

SOURCES OF STRESS

As mentioned earlier, stress arises due to a misfit between environmental demands and personal adequacies to meet these demands. However, management of stress is not possible unless the individual is aware of the specific sources of stress. Stress can emanate from a variety of sources. Pestonjee (1987) contended that one must view the sources of the stress in the light of the social system, to which he belongs.

There are two such systems: the primary system such as family and religion, regional and linguistic groups; and the secondary system such as neighbourhood, schools, colleges, work organizations etc. Pestonjee has identified three important sectors of life in which stress originates. These are (a) Job and Organization (b) Social Sector and (c) Intra-Psychic Sector.

The first, namely, Job and Organization, refers to the totality of the work environment. Cause of stress and unhealthy mental condition of the organizational and industrial workers are varied. Conflicts for power, adverse decision affecting the workers, unhealthy and excessive competition, lot of pressure in work, instability in organizational structure, frequent transfer, misbehavior from the management and colleagues, unhealthy personal relationship with co-workers, frequent quarrels are some of the important causes.

Slight stress is a common experience and stress up to a certain degree help in performance by improving learning. But when conditions of professional work generate high degree of stress in our day to day activities, employees develop various symptoms of anxiety which become harmful to job performance and which affect mental health. On the contrary when there is no stress, due to lack of desire and motivation to perform, performance becomes low.

Secondly, the social sector refers to the social/ cultural context of one's life. It may include religion, caste, language, dress and other such factors. Situational factors, personal factors and Social sactors, produce stress and pollute mental health of industrial and organizational workers.

Massive changes in social structure, generation gap among the young's and olds, gap in communication prestige, recognition in society, traditions and customs prevailing in society containing technological growth, inflation are the social and situational factors producing stress.

Various personal factors like excessive desire for power, desire for self esteem and status, lack of job satisfaction and job security, lack of knowledge about one's performance, economic problems, unrealistically high level of aspiration and personal goal, family problems, divorce and no child, unfavourable relationship with the group are the causes of stress.

Thirdly, the Intra-Psychic Sector encompasses those things which are intimate and personal like temperament, values, abilities and health.

The major organizational stressors are as follows:-

1. **Organizational Policies:-** It provides guidelines for action. Unfavourable and ambiguous policies may affect the functioning of the individuals adversely and they may experience stress.
2. **Organization Structure:-** It provides formal relationships among individuals in an organization. Any defect in organization structure may cause stress. For an example, lack of opportunity of participation in decision making, line and staff conflict etc.

3. **Organizational Process: -** Faulty organizational process like poor communication, inadequate feedback of work performance, ambiguous and conflicting roles cause stress for people in the organization.
4. **Physical Conditions: -** Poor physical conditions like excessive heat and cold, excessive noise, pressure of toxic chemicals and radiation, safely hazards produce stress on people.

Consequences of Stress

Stress can be positive or negative. Positive stress is called EUSTRESS and negative stress is called DISTRESS.

There is a difference between the ways in which Eustress and distress affect the body. Eustress triggers the body alarm, enhances attention, performance and creativity. It has temporary effects. For an example, a person applying for a visa to the US may be under Eustress, and once he/she obtains the visa his/her stress levels come back to normal.

Distress has a negative effect on the body. For example, an individual who has lost his/her job may become depressed which is a result of distress.

Distress can have a serious effect on the body over a period of time.

A certain level of stress can act as a motivator. Without stress, a person becomes lethargic and dull. Eustress encourages a person to perform better. But, if this stress exceeds the resistance level of an individual, it can turn into distress.

Problem Arises Due to Stress

People suffering from stress become very un co-operative, aggressive, quarrelsome and sometimes to avoid stress they become excessive, alcoholic and drugs takers others suffers from repeated illness to be on long leave are remain absent from job.

When the internal body system is unable to tolerate too much stress he may suffer from various diseases. The reactions to stress can be categories under three categories.

1. Physical
2. Psychological
3. Behavioural

1. **Physical** – Heart problem, Insomainia, Joint pain, Indigestion, Blood pressure, Fatigue, Anesia, Cancer, Headache, Asthma, Low immunity.
2. **Psychological** – Depression, Nervous breakdown, ill culture, Suicidal attitude.
3. **Behavioural** – Absenteeism, non co-operation, quarrel-some ness, lack of efficiency, low quality of performance, lack of concentration, irregularity, lack of job satisfaction, frequent changes in job.

Such physical, behavioural and psychological feelings adversely affect the mental health of the workers.

In today's industries and organization due to the repetitive nature of work and specialization in work, job has become very monotonous. Since most part of the work is done by machine and computer, man has to little utilize his brain and initiative. Some low levels of skill are required at the lowest level to manage the work. Their special qualities and creativeness, their intrinsic interest, tact and initiative etc. are not utilized. Thus, a sense of vacuum is created in them and they feel alienated from the job.

The work must be meaningful and motivating requiring tact, initiative, intelligence and creativity. So, the person can have self actualization, conducive for good mental health. The adverse mental health of such person affect their relationship with family members, close associates and friends. In order to avoid such situation, the quality of work should be such that it should be able to satisfying important personal needs of the worker through the job.

Suggestions to Reduce Stress or to Improve 'Mental Health of Employees'

The workers engaged in an organization or industry cannot leave his personal problems with the gate guard and enter into the work space with a true and relaxed mind. He goes there as a total person with all his personal family and sociocultural problem. Socio cultural background, academic qualification, training and past experience, attitude and temperament, all taken together influence him while doing his job. Thus by promoting personal and social satisfaction of the employee, their mental health can be improved. Job satisfaction has to do a lot with mental health of the employees and organizational stress is to be reduced to improve the mental health of the employees.

Following are some suggestions to improve the mental health of employees by reducing overload of stress, anxiety and job dissatisfaction.

1. Career development opportunity but not just a job

Every person has ambition which may be not achieved by doing the job in which the person is already engaged. This type of situation may put him under stress. He should be involved in other activities, which are helpful in achieving their aims.

2. Hobbies

Besides regular paid job one has to keep himself in other self actualization work for relaxation and self-satisfaction. The special and gifted qualities of a person are to be unfolded. He must keep himself engaged in physical exercise like games and sports, painting, reading, singing, playing instrument, gardening, fine arts etc.

3. Involvement in group activities

The individual must make effects to involve himself in group activity as separation from a group leads to loneliness, introversion and day dreaming which are ultimately not conductive for sound mental health by engaging oneself in group activities like puja's, festivals, study tours and eating in groups, one can ease his mental problems.

4. No Excess work

The employee should not be overworked. Enough time should be provided for relaxation. Worker Oriented attitude should be preferred than work oriented attitude.

5. Positive Thinking

Some times a person thinks that he is not capable of doing a particular kind of work. When he failure again and again in doing a particular task, he becomes frustrated from that work. To reduce stress he should develop positive thinking and work hard for doing it.

6. Good Listener

To reduce organizational and formal stress the boss and first line supervisor should be patient listener than a big talker. They should have deep insight into the personal problems of each worker. Face to face contact and direct interaction between the worker and the management is necessary to reduce stress.

7. Stress Management Programs Aids

Counseling session should also be undertaken in every organization to improve mental health. Every possible step should be taken both by the employees themselves and the management to ensure happiness and peace in mind.

There are some other strategies, which are also helpful to reduce the stress. These are:

1. Meditation

Meditation is one of the most effective techniques in reducing and avoiding stress. Regular mediation helps in stress reduction. It

- Enables one to control the thought process.
- Enables one to take effective decisions.
- Helps in physical and mental relaxation.
- Improves concentration.

Meditation is focusing on a single object, thought, syllable (mantra), or experience. If one can attain the mindless state, he/she is said to be in the state of yoga; and this is the key to a stress-free mind. It makes people calm and relaxed. It helps them in dealing with emotions carefully.

2. Yoga

Yoga is another important stress reliever. It simply focuses on gentle postures that improve circulation of blood to vital parts of the body. This increases blood circulation rejuvenates the organs and releases stress. Yogic relaxation is very refreshing and energizing.

3. Holistic therapies

Holistic therapies allow the body to heal naturally. These therapies have no side effects and are reliable. Some popular holistic therapies are message therapy, aromatherapy, reflexology, and nutrition therapy.

Index

F

G

H

I

K

M

N

O

P

R

S